READING NATURE

READING NATURE

The Evolution of American Nature Writing

JOHN SEIBERT FARNSWORTH

MICHIGAN STATE UNIVERSITY PRESS | *East Lansing*

Michigan State University Press
East Lansing, Michigan 48823-5245

LIBRARY OF CONGRESS CATALOGING-IN-PUBLICATION DATA
Names: Farnsworth, John Seibert, author.
Title: Reading nature : the evolution of American nature writing /
John Seibert Farnsworth.
Description: East Lansing : Michigan State University Press, 2025. |
Includes bibliographical references.
Identifiers: LCCN 2024038797 | ISBN 9781611865349 (cloth) |
ISBN 9781611865356 (paperback) | ISBN 9781609177843 |
ISBN 9781628955477
Subjects: LCSH: Ecoliterature, American—History and criticism. |
Nature in literature. | LCGFT: Literary criticism.
Classification: LCC PS163 .F37 2025 |
DDC 810.9/36—dc23/eng/20240827
LC record available at https://lccn.loc.gov/2024038797

Cover design by David Drummond,
Salamander Design, www.salamanderhill.com.

Visit Michigan State University Press at www.msupress.org

Dedicated to Carol

What we always see when we look at nature is our own eyes looking back at us, filtering and altering what we choose to perceive, what we emphasize or ignore, what questions we ask and pursue.

—FRANK STEWARD, *A NATURAL HISTORY OF NATURE WRITING*

Contents

xi   PAYING ATTENTION

1   *Walden; or, Life in the Woods* by Henry David Thoreau (1854)

13   *Land of Little Rain* by Mary Austin (1903)

25   *Ways of Nature* by John Burroughs (1905)

39   *A Sand County Almanac: And Sketches Here and There* by Aldo Leopold (1949)

53   *The Sea Around Us* by Rachel Carson (1951)

65   *Desert Solitaire: A Season in the Wilderness* by Edward Abbey (1968)

77   *Pilgrim at Tinker Creek* by Annie Dillard (1974)

89   *Refuge: An Unnatural History of Family and Place* by Terry Tempest Williams (1991)

101   *Braiding Sweetgrass: Indigenous Wisdom, Scientific Knowledge, and the Teachings of Plants* by Robin Wall Kimmerer (2013)

113   *The Home Place: Memoirs of a Colored Man's Love Affair with Nature*
      by J. Drew Lanham (2016)

125   WRITING NATURE: CONVERGENCES
129   ACKNOWLEDGMENTS
131   WORKS CITED
135   READINGS FOR FURTHER STUDY, BY CHAPTER

Paying Attention

Reading and rereading the works of America's best nature writers, one is tempted to say that there is something in the experience of the American land—or perhaps, the American self in land—that tilts the epistemic and metaphysical underpinnings of historic Western culture and threatens to disturb its modernly dominant logic. —PETER A. FRITZELL, *NATURE WRITING AND AMERICA: ESSAYS UPON A CULTURAL TYPE*

I will not assume, in what follows, that you have read the books examined in this study. While it's great if you've read a few of them, and even better if you pick one up later just to see whether I was right about it, it's not necessary that you've read any of them. My sole exigence in writing this—the reason I picked up the pen in first place—is to explore how our readings of nature have evolved since the publication of Thoreau's *Walden; or, Life in the Woods.*

Here's one important thing this study is not about: I have no intention to propose a canon of literary natural history, a list of works that students, scholars, and devotees of nature writing should have read at some point in their lives. The book in your hands was conceived without the canonical "should," which I've found to be an element of literary criticism that can suck the enjoyment out of the act of reading. I write less as a critic here and more as an author—a fellow nature writer—who is reflecting on how those who have gone before me have influenced what happens whenever I put on my naturalist hat and pick up the pen.

Here's the study's major problem: this book leaves out some of the best nature writing ever to be inked on paper. Some of the more exquisite omissions on my Works Left Out (WLO) list are *Arctic Dreams* by Barry Lopez; *The Pine Island*

Paradox by Kathleen Dean Moore; *The Outermost House* by Henry Beston; *Eating Stone* by Ellen Meloy; *The Desert Year* by Joseph Wood Krutch; *Run, River, Run* by Ann Zwinger; *The Immense Journey* by Loren Eisley; *The Solace of Open Spaces* by Gretel Ehrlich. . . . The list goes on and should no doubt include the fine work of many of my nature-writing friends and mentors, whose writing it would be impossible for me to remain objective about.

The painful thing about my WLO list is that a number of those books are composed of better writing than a few of the works included in this study. The WLO books have not been featured here, however, because they did less to transform the way authors write about nature. While they certainly added to our understanding of the world around us, and most assuredly added to our reading pleasure, in my opinion, the books I've included did more to direct—or sometimes redirect—the focus of our attention as nature writers.

Literary natural history, it turns out, is all about attention.

You may have noticed that I'm going back and forth between "nature writing," the more common way of classifying these texts, and "literary natural history," a more technical descriptor that basically says the same thing. The point of using the term "literary" is to distinguish this type of writing from systematic natural history that is primarily intent on the taxonomic or ethological description of species and their habitats, and from activist writing that is primarily oriented toward the solution of environmental problems. As such, I see the genre having four main characteristics, all of which should be present in some form to qualify as literary natural history:

- The work is attentive to the craft of writing and invokes nature in such a way as to express curiosity and wonder about ecosystems and their inhabitants.
- The work incorporates the naturalist into the text via narratives of personal activity so as to become descriptive of a relationship to nature.
- The work is informed throughout by natural history, as defined by Thomas Fleischner, as "a practice of intentional, focused attentiveness and receptivity to the more-than-human world, guided by honesty and accuracy."
- The work contains an aesthetic, ethical orientation toward nature, especially as regards healthy ecosystems.

Those four characteristics focus on place-based description of local ecosystems, and this may be the list's weakness, for it is not my intention to discriminate here against nature writing that focuses on individual species, such as Sharman Apt Russel's book *Diary of a Citizen Scientist*, which is about her exploits chasing tiger beetles, or Ben Goldfarb's book, *Eager: The Surprising, Secret Life of Beavers and Why They Matter*. Indeed, it would be wrong to be biased against books written about individual animals, such as Lyanda Lynn Haupt's book, *Mozart's Starling*, written about a rescued starling named Carmen. Let's add those excellent books to the list of Works Left Out.

Ten books are reviewed in this study—as it turns out five were written by women and five were written by men. These books appear in the order in which they were published because there is a clear progression in terms of how the observation and description of nature became a dynamic process over the course of 163 years. For the most part, the authors were aware of the nature writing that had come before them, and I have pointed out a few instances where they reference earlier authors found in the study.

In *Walden; or, Life in the Woods*, first published in 1854, Henry David Thoreau filtered his observations of the natural world through a sense of reverence, finding inspiration in how the cycle of the seasons created patterns for all life.

In *Land of Little Rain*, first published in 1903, Mary Hunter Austin expanded our sense of environmental aesthetic so that we might be able to appreciate the beauty of arid landscapes previously scorned as barren, as well as to understand how the desert forms community at both the biotic and cultural levels.

In *Ways of Nature*, first published in 1905, John Burroughs attempted to install an ethic of scientific realism in nature writing as a corrective to a trend toward fantasy and sentimentalism in popular nature stories at the turn of the twentieth century.

In *A Sand County Almanac: And Sketches Here and There*, first published in 1949, Aldo Leopold, adopting an ecological approach, showed us how we fit into the biotic community and taught us the ethical implications of our membership in that community.

In *The Sea Around Us*, first published in 1951, Rachel Carson developed an interdisciplinary ecological aesthetic that would ultimately make it possible—not to mention necessary—for her to write *Silent Spring*.

In *Desert Solitaire: A Season in the Wilderness*, first published in 1968, Edward Abbey critiqued a phenomenon he labelled "industrial tourism," taking a distinct anti-development, anti-government stance and thus situating environmental concern within counter-cultural rhetoric.

In *Pilgrim at Tinker Creek*, first published in 1974, Annie Dillard explored nature as a source of wonder where heightened attention to ecological phenomena could lead to epiphany, a sense of absurdity, and a postmodern awareness of dislocation.

In *Refuge: An Unnatural History of Family and Place*, published in 1991, Terry Tempest Williams integrated the voice of the citizen writer into the field of literary natural history; her narrative linked human health with environmental health through the lived experience of her family.

In *Braiding Sweetgrass: Indigenous Wisdom, Scientific Knowledge, and the Teachings of Plants*, published in 2013, Robin Wall Kimmerer combined scientific and Indigenous ways of knowing the natural world to create a synthesis that can move us beyond environmental despair.

In *The Home Place: Memoirs of a Colored Man's Love of Nature*, published in 2016, J. Drew Lanham explored themes of nature and belonging, joy, and sorrow, while investigating legacies of freedom in an ecosystem where his ancestors were enslaved.

An elevated sense of paying attention runs through all ten of these books. The authors' deep perceptions of the natural world go beyond casual observation and include new ways of investigating the world around them. In every case, this process involved intense levels of emersion into nature, whether by building a cabin, moving into a new biome, going to sea, becoming a park ranger, living a "creek life," monitoring a wildlife reserve, or, more recently, by entering into the realm of nature through the lens of cultural practice.

One other trait these books share is a pathway for exploring landscape. By including the readers in a particular practice of natural history, the better authors take us afield with them, even if it's only for a ramble. When the naturalist author evokes a landscape with skill while narrating the move through that landscape, the reader is able to share in the process of discovery that took place within the site itself. Have I ever gone hiking with Henry Thoreau? Yes, of course I have, even though I was born two months shy of a century after the publication of *Walden*. Indeed, Henry and I have taken the same hike a number of times, and I always seem to learn something new.

The famous nineteenth-century naturalist Louis Agassiz had a sign in his Harvard University lab that instructed his assistants, "Study Nature, Not Books." I had a contrary sign on the door of my office at a university on the other side of the continent, urging students to "Study Nature, Read Books." This experience of reading nature won't take the place of getting out there in person, but it can certainly augment our process of paying attention to the more-than-human world.

Finally, there is something distinctly American about this body of work. On my first pass, I visualized this study as a piece of comparative literature on Anglo-American nature writing. Although I'm a practitioner of American nature writing, I've long been a devotee of British approaches, having earned my doctorate in Scotland and having once taught a course on Anglo-American nature writing on English soil. The deeper I got into the draft, however, the more I became convinced that I was mixing peaches and plums. Despite the common language running through the works I'd selected, a gap was apparent in how writers from our separate continents went about the process of paying attention to nature. It was not that one outlook was superior to the other, just that each gestalt was distinct.

I came to appreciate, in the course of that draft, that there was something distinctive about the American approach: a primal, sublime devotion to the wild that not only differentiates American nature writing, but somehow animates our relationship with the more-than-human world. At the same time, I came to appreciate the growing diversity within American approaches to literary natural history, an expanding range of literary styles, ecological values, and cultural perspectives.

My primary analytical method throughout this study will be close reading, a process of attending to form, context, and style while parsing out meaning. These explications will interrogate how nature writing is as much about the naturalist's personal experience of nature as it is about the natural phenomena being observed or studied. This is an intricate process; while autobiographic accounts of personal experiences will always illustrate the historical moment when the writing took place, the ten works reviewed in this study were often ahead of their times. This quality, to me, is what makes them so interesting.

Here, then, is a close reading of ten works of literary natural history, written by a diverse slate of American writers, that have changed our ways of reading nature.

Walden; or, Life in the Woods by Henry David Thoreau (1854)

> Every man has to learn the points of the compass again as often as he awakes, whether from sleep or any abstraction. —FROM THE CHAPTER, "THE VILLAGE"

In 1817, James Madison was sworn in as the fifth president of the United States, the Mississippi territory was admitted as the twentieth U.S. state, the First Seminole War began in Florida, and Baltimore became the first U.S. city to install gas streetlights. Jane Austen died that year, and her novel, *Persuasion*, was published posthumously. The young Ralph Waldo Emerson matriculated to Harvard College in 1817, and Henry David Thoreau was born in Concord, Massachusetts.

A week shy of his twenty-eighth birthday, on the Fourth of July of 1845, Thoreau moved into a cabin he'd built on Walden Pond as part of a social experiment but also to write a book, his first book. That book was not the classic we all know as *Walden*. Rather, it would ultimately be published as *A Week on the Concord and Merrimack Rivers*, a narrative about a river trip he had taken six years earlier with his brother, John, from Concord, Massachusetts, to Concord, New Hampshire. John Thoreau had died of tetanus in his younger brother's arms at the age of twenty-seven, and his brother, Henry, wrote the book about their river trip as a tribute to John's memory. This is a point that many scholars miss: Thoreau's impetus for the Walden project was not to write a book about his solitary adventure in the woods. His writerly goal for those two years was to memorialize a brother for whom he still grieved.

During his time living on Walden Pond, Henry kept a journal, an ongoing project begun in 1837 at the suggestion of Ralph Waldo Emerson. This journal ultimately comprised over two million words and forty-seven manuscript volumes and was completed in 1861, shortly before his death from tuberculosis at the age of forty-four. It was from his journal notes that he ultimately wrote the book, *Walden; or, Life in the Woods*, which was published in 1854, seven years after Thoreau had concluded his experiment living on Walden Pond. But that book was clearly an afterthought.

In his 1948 biography of Thoreau, Joseph Wood Krutch, one of the more prolific of America's forgotten nature writers, wrote: "In other words, the over-all shape of the book preserves the main outlines of the thing it professes to be: not an argument but an account of the somewhat eccentric experiment concerning which Thoreau's neighbors had expressed a curiosity." Indeed, the first three chapters originated as lectures given at the Concord Lyceum, lectures that had been specifically requested by Thoreau's neighbors. The people of Concord genuinely wanted to know what he'd been up to for two years, and why. Thoreau wasn't writing to encourage the rest of humanity to follow his example; he was merely describing his experience and passing along some reading recommendations.

Unfortunately, Thoreau doesn't tell us what this experiment was about until sixty pages into the book, when he writes, famously, "I went to the woods because I wished to live deliberately, to front only the essential facts of life, and see if I could not learn what it had to teach, and not, when I came to die, discover that I had not lived."

Thoreau essentially set out on a two-year retreat where the first step was to build a cabin within which the retreat would be conducted, and the second would be to grow the food upon which he could subsist. This was not a naive project.

Thoreau was not following a prototype established by anyone else writing about nature. He opted, for example, to devote his first chapter to a discourse on economics. Early on he takes up the role of provocateur, writing: "I see young men, my townsmen, whose misfortune it is to have inherited farms, houses, barns, cattle, and farming tools; for these are more easily acquired than got rid of. Better if they had been born in the open pasture and suckled by a wolf, that they might have seen with clearer eyes what field they were called to labor in."

The reader will soon learn that when Thoreau is writing in a naturalistic vein his observations will be as straightforward as they are keen, and his mode of cataloguing the natural world will tend to be conventional. His examination of society will be highly critical, however, starting with the observation, "The mass of men lead lives of quiet desperation." The perceptive reader comes to understand that Thoreau seems ready to question every part of the traditional social order and that natural processes will become a standard for seeking out the truth. For example, in the first chapter, he discusses the farmer who insists, "You cannot live on vegetable food solely, for it furnishes nothing to make bones with." This same farmer, Thoreau points out, spends the day plowing behind his oxen, "which, with vegetable-made bones, jerk him and his lumbering plow along in spite of every obstacle." Nature wins the argument, and it always shall as far as Thoreau is concerned.

Thoreauvian economics are fairly straightforward. Some of what society has come to see as necessity is actually luxury; we pay the cost for that luxury by needing to labor longer and longer hours. If we are able to simplify, we will in turn be able to invest time into our betterment. In Thoreau's words, "Most of the luxuries, and many of the so-called comforts of life, are not only not indispensable, but positive hindrances to the elevation of mankind. With respect to luxuries and comforts, the wisest have ever lived a more simple and meagre life than the poor." For Thoreau, the time not spent in the pursuit of luxury is re-budgeted in favor of practicing natural history.

Thoreau does not leave this conversation on the level of philosophical debate but follows through with its practical application by building the cabin himself. To begin, he hewed his main timbers, six inches square, as well as the studs, rafters, and floor timbers, all from pine, all using an axe by hand rather than buying milled wood. Then he purchased the shanty of an immigrant laborer who had worked on the Fitchburg Railroad, paying $4.25 for the boards and hauling them away himself after dismantling the shanty. He dug his cellar by hand, framed the house "with the help of some acquaintances," and moved in before building the fireplace, which was crafted of stone that he gathered himself from the edges of the pond. Before winter the chimney was built, and Thoreau shingled the sides of his house with "imperfect and sappy singles made of the first slice of the log, whose edges I was obliged to straighten with a plane." At the conclusion of all this he wrote: "I have thus a tight shingled and plastered house, ten feet wide by fifteen long, and eight-feet posts, with a garret and a closet, a large window on each side, two trap doors, one door at the end, and a brick fireplace opposite."

Here Thoreau itemized all his expenses for raw materials, including two casks of lime for $2.40—to which he adds "That was high"—for a total cost of $28.12½. By way of comparison, Thoreau points out that at the college he'd attended, "the mere rent of a student's room, which is only little larger than my own, is thirty dollars each year." This, of course, diverges into a discourse about education where Thoreau suggests that it may be better, when a new college is being built, for the students to lay the foundation themselves.

Thoreau also pointed out that the railroad fare to Fitchburg, which was thirty miles away, was ninety cents, which represented a day's wages. Thus, he could get to Fitchburg more quickly by walking there in a day than by working a day to earn the fare and then taking the train the next day. Employing this sort of logic, he was able to conclude his discussion of economics by stating that he could meet his living expenses by working about six weeks a year, which would give him the whole of his winters, as well as most of his summers, free and clear for study. He accomplished this, of course, by living simply.

A good deal of the fun in teaching Walden to modern-day students is coming to the collective realization at how much society has changed since the day when the average laborer made ninety cents per day. On the other hand, I've noticed that a few of the chapters are difficult for contemporary students to access because Thoreau inhabited an intellectual milieu so divergent from that of today. The third chapter, simply titled "Reading," is a good example of this, especially given the preponderance of classical reading matter Thoreau reflects upon. My students have been genuinely puzzled as to why anyone would include a chapter on reading the classics in a book about a two-year experiment living closer to nature. One has to remind them that Thoreau lived in a world devoid of video games, television, radio, recorded music, social media, internet news, and everything more technologically innovative than a hand-printed newspaper, the likes of which he'd have to go into town to procure. Thoreau assumes that his readers will understand the importance of reading, noting only in passing that his residence was more favorable to serious reading than a university. Of course there should be a chapter on reading early on in *Walden*! To today's university student, this is revelatory, and, when they reflect on the amount of time Thoreau must have spent reading out there in the woods, the lack of alternative entertainment can seem oppressive.

To my view, it is in his fourth chapter that Thoreau finally begins to evoke nature in earnest. In a single long sentence, he is able to share the depth of his observations in a given moment:

> As I sit at my window this summer afternoon, hawks are circling about my clearing; the tantivy of wild pigeons, flying by two and threes athwart

my view, or perching restless on the white pine boughs behind my house, gives a voice to the air; a fish hawk dimples the glassy surface of the pond and brings up a fish; a mink steals out of the marsh before my door and seizes a frog by the shore; the sedge is bending under the weight of the reed-birds flitting hither and thither; and for the last half-hour I have heard the rattle of railroad cars, now dying away and then reviving like the beat of a partridge, conveying travellers from Boston to the country.

We learn a great deal more about the Fitchburg Railroad in the next few paragraphs, beginning with the revelation that it "touches the pond about a hundred rods south of where I dwell," (in other words, about half a kilometer away.) Contrary to what we might expect, Thoreau does not seem at all put out about civilization encroaching so closely on his retreat. Indeed, the technology of harnessing steam and putting it at the service of commerce impresses him, as does the regularity of its passing. He notes that "to do things 'railroad fashion' is now the byword." Speaking of the train's whistle, he opines that "it is worth the while to be warned so often and so sincerely by any power to get off its track." From my Anthropocene perspective, I want to detect a note of sarcasm, or at least irony, in Thoreau's musings about the Fitchburg Railroad, but I fear that his enthusiasm is genuine.

The two chapters that follow, "Solitude" and "Visitors," seem on the surface to be strangely juxtaposed. In the first, Thoreau describes the depth of the solitude available to him, telling the reader, famously, "I find it wholesome to be alone the greater part of the time. To be in company, even with the best, is soon wearisome and dissipating. I love to be alone. I never found the companion that was so companionable as solitude." The next chapter contains his equally famous line, "I had three chairs in my house; one for solitude, two for friendship, three for society." To this he adds that, when there were more than three visitors, those without a chair would "economize the room by standing up." We understand from secondary sources that there were often more people visiting the cabin than there were chairs for them.

Judging from the reactions of former students, any number of readers would prefer Thoreau to favor one or the other, solitude or society. One young scholar, reacting to Thoreau's sentence, "I am no more lonely than the Mill Brook, or a weathercock, or the north star, or the south wind, or an April shower, or a January thaw, or the first spider in a new house," responded that of course Thoreau wasn't lonely; he had a constant stream of visitors keeping him company, and he ate Sunday dinners with his family every week.

While it's natural for the reader to want Thoreau to make up his mind between solitude and society, without him saying so directly it seems that what he really enjoyed was the balance that this experiment in the woods afforded him. Solitude became normative enough for Thoreau to feel that "every little pine needle expanded and swelled with sympathy and befriended me." At the same time, human interaction was infrequent enough that it provided a break from the routine rather than being itself routine. As Thoreau observed, "Society is commonly too cheap. We meet at very short intervals, not having had time to acquire any new value for each other. We meet at meals three times a day, and give each other a new taste of that old musty cheese that we are. We have had to agree on a certain set of rules, called etiquette and politeness, to make this frequent meeting tolerable and that we need not come to open war."

By the time we get to the seventh chapter, "The Bean Field," Thoreau has already mentioned his beans a dozen times, beginning with how they contributed to the economy of his endeavor. It's enough that a former student once asked, "What's with Thoreau and his beans?" Thoreau's answer, and here I'm simplifying by removing the allusions to Greek mythology, is simply that they attached him to the earth.

The more Thoreau established himself in the woods, the more curious he seemed about the goings-on in the village. In the chapter by that name, "The Village," he writes: "Every day or two I strolled to the village to hear some of the gossip which is incessantly going on there, circulating either from mouth to mouth, or from newspaper to newspaper, and which, taken in homeopathic doses, was really as refreshing in its way as the rustle of leaves and the peeping of frogs." Note that he is viewing the village from the outside, making similar observations about village gossip as when he listens to wild phenomena such as the peeping of frogs. He hears with different ears: when the naturalist returns to civilization, he does not stop making the sort of observations that naturalists make. I have felt this same phenomenon when returning home after protracted field experiences: I continue observing behaviors through similar lenses as before, even though my "subjects," as it were, are no longer wild flora and fauna.

The sense of being present but estranged is amplified, toward the end of the chapter, when Thoreau reveals that once, when he was in town to pick a mended shoe up at the cobblers, he was thrown into jail. This happened because of his refusal to pay a tax as a protest against recognizing the authority of "the State which buys and sells men, women, and children, like cattle, at the door of its senate-house."

Thoreau notes the irony that he is less safe in town than in the woods, where "I had no lock or bolt for the desk which held my papers, nor even a nail to put over my latch or windows. I never fastened my door night or day, even when I was to be absent several days."

Thoreau had sufficient confidence as a developing naturalist to describe features of natural history about which he was perplexed or baffled. In one example of this, from a chapter titled "The Ponds," he describes clear rings, near Walden's sandy eastern shore, where, from a boat in water ten feet deep, they appear as "circular heaps half a dozen feet in diameter by a foot in height, consisting of small stones less than a hen's egg in size, where all around is bare sand." After speculating about possible origins of these rings, he confesses, "I know not by what fish they could be made. Perhaps they are the nests of the chivin. They lend a pleasing mystery to the bottom." In this case, Thoreau was correct in his speculations: the mystery fish turns out to be the chivin, more commonly known these days as "fallfish," *Semotilus corporalis*, the largest minnow species native to eastern North America.

Thoreau reflects on hunting as a youthful pastime, noting that "almost every New England boy among my contemporaries shouldered a fowling piece between the ages of ten and fourteen." He writes that "when at the pond I wished sometimes to add fish to my fare for variety," but at that point he had outgrown fowling. Then comes his confession for having kept his gun too many years: "As for fowling, during the last years that I carried a gun my excuse was that I was studying ornithology, and sought only new or rare birds. But I confess that I am now inclined to think that there is a finer way of studying ornithology than this. It requires so much closer attention to the habits of the birds, that, if for that reason only, I have been willing to omit the gun."

Thoreau was more than a century ahead of his time when he wrote this. In his day, it was a point of honor among ornithologists not to identify a specimen unless they'd shot it and examined it by hand. This explains the archaic-seeming names of many bird species such as the sharp-shinned hawk, the sharpness of the shins only being identifiable if the bird is in hand. It wasn't until the 1960's that questions emerged in ornithological literature as to whether the use of optics, especially cameras, as well as sound recordings could be a way to confirm and legitimatize an ornithological observation. Indeed, a debate about the need to continue collecting specimens for natural history museums persists to this day.

Thoreau doesn't condemn hunting entirely and thinks of it as a healthy way for boys to get oriented to the outdoors. While hunting provides an introduction to the forest, Thoreau sees a natural progression: "He goes thither at first as a hunter and fisher, until at last, if he has the seeds of a better life in him, he distinguishes his proper objects, as a poet or naturalist it may be, and leaves the gun and fish-pole behind." In Thoreau's case, he has not yet made this transition 100 percent, stating, "There is unquestionably this instinct in me which belongs to the lower orders of creation; yet with every year I am less a fisherman, though without more humanity or even wisdom; at present I am no fisherman at all." This is confusing, because he speaks of fishing during his time living at Walden Pond, but I assume that when he writes "at present" he is referencing the time of his writing the book six or seven years after the fact. Clearly, the point came in his life where he preferred a vegetarian option, claiming that abstaining from animal food preserved his "higher or poetic faculties." If nothing else, it was one more opportunity for him to simplify his lifestyle.

When ice finally formed on the pond, Thoreau experimented with how bubbles form in the ice. With winter's arrival, he writes graciously that "at length the winter set in good earnest, just as I had finished plastering, and the wind began to howl around the house as if it had not had permission to do so till then." As the snow continues to fall and the ice finally covers the entire pond, Thoreau writes, "I withdrew yet farther into my shell, and endeavored to keep a bright fire both within my house and within my breast." He was to spend more and more time collecting firewood at this point, finally composing my favorite line in the book: "Every man looks at his wood-pile with a kind of affection." Yes, my woodpile knows that look.

Despite his success at gathering wood, including an old, blown-down fence and stumps that were left behind after others cut firewood on their woodlots, Thoreau is aware that he is denuding the forest of deadwood and, in an effort to warm his cabin more sustainably, tells us, "The next winter I used a small cooking-stove for economy, since I did not own the forest; but it did not keep fire so well as the open fireplace. Cooking was then, for the most part, no longer a poetic, but merely a chemic process. . . . The stove not only took up room and scented the house, but it concealed the fire, and I felt as if I had lost a companion. You can always see a face in the fire."

There is an intimacy here that I feel as a reader for the author, and this feeling bears examination. Thoreau tells me, almost confessionally, that much of the romance goes out of warming his house and cooking his food when, for reasons of thrift, he demotes his fire to a cooking stove, thus constricting it, rather than using the open fireplace which is much less frugal with firewood. He clearly understands why he must do this and yet confesses that he feels as if he lost a companion during the cold winter nights when he must have felt most alone. So here we have a man who seems to write up his experience in total honesty, whether he feels a wild urge to chase down a woodchuck and devour it raw, or whether the dream house he writes of is almost the antithesis of the simple, economic cabin that hosts his experiment, or when he complains of a feeling of lost companionship when he abandons his hand-built fireplace for a more frugal cooking stove. Thoreau is allowing us inside his head even when his thoughts aren't at their transcendental apex. Compare this with Emerson, his mentor as a writer, who seems to strive for a constant nobility of thought, nobility fortified with moral purpose. But it's important for Thoreau to write with stark honesty because it is integral to the book's undertaking. He wrote this book not only because his neighbors want to know what the experiment was trying to prove but also because they wanted to know what it was like being out there during his time in the woods. Thoreau lets us know that it wasn't all birdsong and huckleberries.

The fourteenth chapter, "Former Inhabitants and Winter Visitors," is receiving greater scrutiny these days because many of the previous inhabitants of the woods around Walden Pond were either enslaved or formerly enslaved. Walden Woods became a refuge for Black people, who had few other options to live as emancipated people, because, prior to the passage of the fourteenth amendment to the U.S. Constitution, adopted in 1868, formerly enslaved people were not considered U.S. citizens even if they had been born in the United States. Technically, they were considered foreigners and were thus not afforded basic civil rights. During Thoreau's lifetime, for example, they would not have been permitted to own property in the town of Concord. Such restrictions applied even to men who had been granted their freedom as the result of serving in the Continental Army during the American Revolution.

The Black community within Walden Woods had dispersed before Thoreau took up residence. He wrote that "for human society I was obliged to conjure up the former occupants of these woods." But he did more than conjure them up; he researched their lives in enough depth to provide at least a one-paragraph biography on many of these formerly enslaved residents, noting what remained of their dwellings and their orchards. Thoreau thus ensures that their occupation of the Walden Woods will be considered part of the heritage of that place, even though by the time he built his cabin whatever encampment had previously been there was no longer active. A contributing factor in this, according to historian Elise Lemire's book *Black Walden*, was that many of them died of hunger, because it was difficult to grow enough protein in the agriculturally poor soil of the woods surrounding Walden Pond. Thoreau pondered, unsuccessfully, the reason for the community's failure, asking "But this small village, germ of something more, why did it fail while Concord keeps its ground?" He seems to think that it could have succeeded, but this may be an area where he is unaware of his own privilege as a white citizen.

The chapter "Winter Animals" functions as a grand soundscape where whatever loss of visual observation may have been caused by the diminished light of winter is more than made up for by Thoreau's acoustic perspective. He begins composing his soundscape by noting his distance from the jingle of sleigh bells whenever he travels during winter, and then states: "For sounds in winter nights, and often in winter days, I heard the forlorn but melodious note of a hooting owl indefinitely far; such a sound as the frozen earth would yield if struck with a suitable plectrum, the very lingua vernacula of Walden Wood, and quite familiar to me at last, though I never saw the bird while it was making it." He claims that he seldom opened his door without hearing a sonorous, "Hoo hoo hoo, hoorer, hoo." He moves on quickly to the loud honking of geese, describing "the sound of their wings like a tempest in the woods as they flew low over my house." Thoreau goes on to claim that he could sometimes hear foxes "as they ranged over the snow-crust, in moonlight nights, in search of a partridge or other game, barking raggedly and demoniacally like forest dogs, as if laboring with some anxiety." He also states that "sometimes one came near to my window, attracted by my light, barked a vulpine curse at me, and then retreated."

Thoreau is clearly having fun with this chapter. He describes having thrown a half bushel of sweet corn that had failed to ripen out his window to see what creatures would be drawn to it. There were squirrels and rabbits, of course, but later the jays arrived, "whose discordant screams were heard long before, as they were warily making their approach an eighth of a mile off, and in a stealthy and sneaking manner they flit from tree to tree, nearer and nearer, and pick up the kernels which the squirrels have dropped." One realizes, at that point, the acoustic irony in calling the approach of the jays "stealthy."

Spring arrives, finally, in the seventeenth chapter. Thoreau writes that "one attraction in coming to the woods to live was that I should have leisure and opportunity to see the Spring come in." A devotee of phenology, keeping careful records of the seasonal arrivals of flora and fauna, he notes that he is "on the alert for the first signs of spring, to hear the chance note of some arriving bird, or the striped squirrel's chirp, for his stores must be now nearly exhausted, or see the woodchuck venture out of his winter quarters." In his journals, he records such things as when the ice breaks up on the pond, and when the first sparrow of spring shows up, and when "the grass flames up on the hillside like a spring fire."

By the end of this chapter, Thoreau has taken his readers through an entire solar year that started with summer and concludes the following spring. But having captured the seasons in prose, he has no intention of doing so again, concluding this chapter where he has been so grandiloquent about the virtues of spring almost tersely: "Thus was my first year's life in the woods completed; and the second year was similar to it. I finally left Walden September 6th, 1847."

Had I been Thoreau's editor, I would have encouraged him to throw out the first seven paragraphs of his conclusion. His point seems to be that the universe is wider than our views of it, a point that doesn't seem to need arguing. Moreover, his paragraphs about explorations of the Mississippi, the Nile, the South Seas, et cetera, make it seem as if he is dissatisfied with where he has been. Once the reader has slogged through those paragraphs, however, a rationale appears. Thoreau writes, "I left the woods for as good a reason as I went there." But we are left on our own to remember that his initial quest was to live deliberately and to see whether he could learn what the woods had to teach. So the question, ultimately, must be "What did you learn?"

Thoreau doesn't leave us in the lurch on this question, telling us, famously, "I learned this, at least, by my experiment: that if one advances confidently in the direction of his dreams, and endeavors to live the life which he has imagined, he will meet with a success unexpected in common hours."

The critical prompt here, in the end, was to reiterate that it had been an experiment. Experiments must come to a close to have value, for the benefit is in conclusions that can only be drawn once an experiment has culminated. For Thoreau, there was never a question about his connection with nature—where he needed a deeper connection was in his relationship with society. By spending two years in the woods, largely taking a break from society, he was able to identify what parts of social interaction were of importance to him. Thus, when he concludes that he left the woods for as good a reason as he went there, we must assume that he took with him a renewed vision of how he was to fit into the ecosystem of Concord, which never stopped being his home despite the two years on Walden Pond.

To fully understand the book, we must understand that it is not a manifesto. Rather, it is a description of a profound experience after reflecting for years about its significance. Ironically, nature is the place where Henry David Thoreau ultimately discerned his role in society. Part of that role was to be the naturalist who can help society appreciate the natural world aesthetically. The other part is to be a social critic who can advocate for his readers to simplify their lives. After the Walden experiment, he had much to say in both regards.

Thoreau's honesty in terms of his time at Walden Pond, especially regarding the times where he shares what was going on inside his head, not only revolutionizes nature writing, but changes how we look at nature. The book is not fundamentally about the naturalist advancing science, as was the case with those who practiced natural history prior to Thoreau. Regardless of whether he identified new phenomena, *Walden Pond* is more about just being there, out in the woods. This is a whole new way to value the experience of being in nature: what's most important is to spend time there, attentively, waiting for whatever comes next, waiting with faith that capital-n Nature will take care of the details as each season becomes the next.

Land of Little Rain by Mary Austin (1903)

Once at Red Rock, in a year of green pasture, which is a bad time for the scavengers, we saw two buzzards, five ravens, and a coyote feeding on the same carrion, and only the coyote seemed ashamed of the company. —FROM THE CHAPTER, "THE SCAVENGERS"

In 1868, the Fourteenth Amendment to the U.S. Constitution was adopted, guaranteeing citizenship for African Americans. President Andrew Johnson, having faced impeachment earlier that year, granted unconditional pardon to all Civil War rebels, and the states of Florida, Alabama, Louisiana, Georgia, North Carolina, and South Carolina were readmitted to the union. That same year, the Treaty of Fort Laramie was brokered by General William Tecumseh Sherman, thus ending a policy of total war on all Indigenous nations of the Great Plains. The Wyoming Territory was organized. The first volume of Louisa May Alcott's novel, *Little Women*, was published, and Mary Hunter Austin was born in Carlinville, Illinois.

There is a Presbyterian college in Carlinville, Blackburn College, where Mary Hunter studied botany and received her degree in 1888, shortly before her twentieth birthday. Reflecting later in an essay titled "Woman Alone," she wrote, "I won a college degree by dint of insisting on it, and by crowding its four years into two and a half while my brother had the full four years." Her family moved west shortly after she graduated, setting up a homestead in the San Joaquin Valley in California. From there, once married she would move to the Owens Valley in the arid eastern Sierra, where her husband, Stafford Wallace Austin, would speculate unsuccessfully in water rights.

Despite the distinction of being a woman with a college degree at the close of the nineteenth century, Austin had difficulty establishing herself as a teacher and, for that matter, passing the licensing exam. Regardless of early career setbacks, she would go on to write thirty-three books, three plays, and to publish hundreds of articles and poems. Most notable among her corpus was her 1903 masterwork, *Land of Little Rain*.

Austin begins her narrative by interrogating a frontier notion of "desert," describing it thus in the second paragraph of her first chapter: "Desert is a loose term to indicate land that supports no man; whether the land can be bitted and broken to that purpose is not proven. Void of life it never is, however dry the air and villainous the soil." The metaphor here, comparing the desert landscape to a horse that has not been trained to accept a bit or a rider, suggests that the desert has not been tamed. This sets up a polarity between the domestic and the wild throughout the book, one that the author deconstructs playfully, alternately portraying the wild in the domestic, and the domestic in the wild. While she can't escape the wild-west portrayal of landscape that will engage her readers, at the same time she undertakes to evoke the desert's beauty in tender ways.

Even as late as the dawn of the twentieth century, the prevailing concept of desert among non-Indigenous people came from Judeo-Christian scriptures, which in the book of Deuteronomy framed it as "a barren and howling waste." But Austin introduces a twist early in her account when she points out that the desert is never devoid of life. She immediately takes on a role as the desert's apologist, stating, for example, that there are many areas in the desert where drinkable water lies within a few feet of the surface, and claiming that "the tragedy of desert deaths" could have been avoided in places like Death Valley, which earned its name when a pioneer perished while attempting to cross in a wagon train. From Austin's perspective, the problem with aridity lies not with the desert itself but with ignorance, especially in terms of settlers who don't understand desert ways.

Austin is acutely aware of her audience's expectations of a woman writing about desert natural history. She reflects that "is it not perhaps to satisfy expectation that one falls into the tragic key in writing of desertness? The more you wish of it the more you get, and in the mean time lose much of the pleasantness." In short, she realizes that her readers expect narratives of heat, danger, harshness, and tribulation. She no doubt could fill the book with tales of desert troubles and tragedies, and yet she wants the reader to know of the aesthetic delights of desert dwelling. She wants them to know of the clean air, the star-filled nights, "the rainbow hills, the tender bluish mists, the luminous radiance of the spring."

On the surface level, there seem to be contradictions in Austin's appraisal of the land, and the astute reader will eventually discern that the author understands the landscape to generate paradox. She makes statements such as, "A land of lost rivers, with little in it to love; yet a land that once visited must be come back to inevitably." Her appraisal of the landscape's vitality tends to be emotional and subjective, never economic.* Austin is convinced of the land's agency, its ability to shape the ecological and cultural communities within it. More than once in the book, she makes the point that the land will not be lived in except in its own fashion. This rule applies not only to flora and fauna but to humans as well.

Austin's descriptions of the natural world border on the mystical; she writes from the perspective of someone who has watched and listened intently while perceiving the unknowable on an animal level. Notice the interplay between seeing, hearing, and feeling in this passage from the chapter "The Mesa Trail":

> In quiet weather mesa days have no parallel for stillness, but the night silence breaks into certain mellow or poignant notes. Late afternoons the burrowing owls may be seen blinking at the doors of their hummocks with perhaps four or five elfish nestlings arow, and by twilight begin a soft *woo-oo-ing*, rounder, sweeter, more incessant in mating time. It is not possible to disassociate the call of the burrowing owl from the late slant light of the mesa. If the fine vibrations which are the golden-violet glow of spring twilights were to tremble into sound, it would be just that mellow double note breaking along the blossom-tops.

Austin evokes a romantic soundscape, all the more notable given the fact that her imagination makes it possible to convert the "fine vibrations" of the visible light spectrum into sound, suggesting that twilight would approximate the hoots of owls. There is fantasy here, certainly, and yet it is the product of keen observation on multiple levels.

Austin is sympathetic to Indigenous culture throughout the book and spent significant amounts of time researching native practices and lore. The following paragraph from the chapter "Shoshone Land" exemplifies the rigor of her research,

---

* Extractive industry was flourishing during the time Austin composed *The Land of Little Rain*. Not only was there a resurgence of gold mining, but there was a boom in the number of borax mines opening, a boom that would last until 1907, three years after the book was published.

especially where it becomes obvious that she sampled Shoshone cuisine prior to writing about it, a fact that may have shocked her readers:

> As for food, that appears to be chiefly a matter of being willing. Desert Indians all eat chuck-wallas, big black and white lizards that have delicate white flesh savored like chicken. Both the Shoshones and the coyotes are fond of the flesh of *Gopherus agazzazii*, the turtle that by feeding on buds, going without drink, and burrowing in the sand through the winter, contrives to live a known period of twenty-five years. It seems that most seeds are foodful in the arid regions, most berries are edible, and many shrubs good for firewood with the sap in them. The mesquite bean, boiled to a kind of mush, and dried in cakes, sulphur-colored and needing an axe to cut it, is an excellent food for long journeys. Fermented in water with wild honey and the honeycomb, it makes a pleasant, mildly intoxicating drink.

Austin constructs nature in this paragraph as being providential. Nature cares for every need, even inebriation, providing that its wild domesticity is understood outside the vagaries of civilized fashion.

In addition to her empathy for the Indigenous people living in the land of little rain, Austin admires others who have settled into the place: miners; cattlemen; mule-team drivers; sheep herders; circuit-riding preachers; prospectors, which Austin calls "pocket hunters"; and even a faro dealer.* Early in the book, she reflects, "If one is inclined to wonder at first how so many dwellers came to be in the loneliest land that ever came out of God's hands, what they do here and why they stay, one does not wonder so much after having lived here." She realizes that the lure of striking it rich is part of the formula but ultimately feels that desert aesthetics trump everything else. She writes of a mule-team driver, Salty Williams, who once quit his job, complaining that it was "too durn hot." She reported seeing him later once again up in the driver's seat, "tanned and ruddy as a harvest moon, looking through the golden dust above his eighteen mules. The land had called him."

On the nonhuman side of the animal kingdom, Austin pays greater attention to the coyote than any other desert dweller. *Canis latrans*, referenced at one point

---

* Faro is a game of chance once popular in the American West that is no longer played in casinos as of this writing. In the early 1900s, faro was replaced by poker as the game of choice among gamblers. Although faro was easier to learn than poker, it was much easier for a dealer, who controlled the game's bank, to cheat via sleight of hand.

as "your real lord of the mesa," is described affectionately in several chapters. "This short-legged meat-eater," Austin observes clinically, "loves half lights and lowering days, has no friends, no enemies, and disowns his offspring." She writes with admiration that "the coyote is the true water-witch, one who snuffs and paws, snuffs and paws again at the smallest spot of moisture-scented earth until he has freed the blind water from the soil." She states that she has trailed a coyote cross-country often, watching it head toward where "some slant-winged scavenger hanging in the air signaled the prospect of a dinner." But a few pages later, she explains that a coyote is not a scavenger by choice, "but being on the whole a lazy dog, is apt to fall into carrion eating because it is easier." Clearly, Austin is not trying to espouse the scientific detachment usually affected by natural historians of her day but approaches her subjects with endearment and empathy.

Ultimately, the modern reader may gain more from Austin's notes regarding culture than her forays into natural history. She depicts human culture with a fresh accuracy, both in terms of Indigenous people and settlers, and can be read as a window into the times in the region. While today she is regarded as an early feminist, as well as a defender of Native American and Mexican American rights, for the most part her political commentary was written after *Land of Little Rain* was published.

Despite Austin's admiration for how the Indigenous people coexisted with desert ecology, she is critical of abandoned campoodies.† She writes, "It takes man to leave unsightly scars on the face of the earth. Here on the mesa the abandoned campoodies of the Paiutes are spots of desolation long after the wattles of the huts have warped in the brush heaps." Notwithstanding, the paragraph that follows contains a description of an active encampment that might be of interest to modern anthropologists:

> A campoodie at noontime, when there is no smoke rising and no stir of life, resembles nothing so much as a collection of prodigious wasps' nests. The huts are squat and brown and chimneyless, facing east, and the inhabitants have the faculty of quail for making themselves scarce in the underbrush at the approach of strangers. But they are really not often at home during midday, only the blind and incompetent left to keep the camp. These are

---

† "Campoodie" references a non-permanent encampment that functioned as a temporary village for multiple families. It was probably a pidgin term, and in later books Austin reverts to the Spanish term, *campoda*.

working hours, and all across the mesa one sees the women whisking seeds of *chia* into their spoon-shaped baskets, these emptied again into the huge conical carriers, supported on the shoulders by a leather band about the forehead.

Austin dedicates an entire chapter to "Shoshone Land," which begins with a boast that "it is true that I have been in Shoshone Land." She describes this land as "the country of the bighorn, the wapiti,* and the wolf, nesting place of buzzards, land of cloud-nourished trees and wild things that live without drink. Above all, it is the land of the creosote and the mesquite." What she doesn't tell us is that it's located in the Mojave Desert, a place name she uses elsewhere in the book. Her directions on how to get there would be difficult for the modern traveler to follow:

> To reach that country . . . one goes south and south, within hearing of the lip-lip-lapping of the great tideless lake, and south by east over a high rolling district, miles and miles of sage and nothing else. So one comes to the country of the painted hills,—old red cones of craters, wasteful beds of mineral earths, hot, acrid springs, and steam jets issuing from a leprous soil. After the hills the black rock, after the craters of spewed lava, ash strewn, of incredible thickness, and full of sharp, winding rifts. There are picture writings carved deep in the face of the cliffs to mark the way for those who do not know it. On the very edge of the black rock the earth falls away in a wide sweeping hollow, which is Shoshone Land.

The mysticism of Mary Austin is at times subtle and at other times borders on the pietistic. Either way, she has clearly moved beyond the Methodism to which she had converted as an adolescent. In most cases, Austin's mysticism is triggered when she evokes sky, wind, clouds, or stars. It would not be inaccurate to classify her theology as constructing a "sky religion." In more subtle moments, she will write something along the lines of, "Out West, the west of the mesas and the unpatented hills, there is more sky than any place in the world. It does not sit flatly on the rim of the earth, but begins somewhere out in the space in which the earth is poised, hollows more, and is full of clean winey winds." In more pious terms, she observes that "for all the toll the desert takes of a man it gives compensations, deep breaths,

---

* Austin uses *wapiti*, the Shawnee name for *Cervus canadensis*, also commonly known as the American elk. The Shawnee term literally means "white rump."

deep sleep, and the communion of the stars." In a few instances, she goes so far as to sound dogmatic, as in: "The first effect of cloud study is the presence and intention in storm processes. Weather does not happen. It is the visible manifestation of the Spirit moving itself in the void."

Also peeking through her writing, here and there, is a dry wit. This sometimes comes out as social commentary, and other times emerges as a wry reflection on human nature. In a chapter called "The Mesa Trail," she develops one shepherd's character thus: "Petite Pete, who works a circuit up from the Ceriso to Red Butte and around by way of Salt Flats, passes year by year on the mesa trail, his thick hairy chest thrown open to all weathers, twirling his long staff, and dealing brotherly with his dogs, who are possibly as intelligent, certainly handsomer."

The chapter on a mining town, named "Jimville," stands out as a particular comedy, starting with the means of arriving there. Austin writes, "The road to Jimville is the happy hunting ground of old stage-coaches brought up from superseded routes the West over, rocking, lumbering, wide vehicles far gone in the odor of romance, coaches that Vasquez has held up, from whose high seats express messengers have shot or have been shot as their luck held. This is to comfort you when the driver stops to rummage for a wire to mend a failing bolt."

My favorite anecdote from the Jimville chapter relates to a church fair that was held at the Silver Dollar saloon as a benefit for the circuit rider, "who preached to the few that would hear, and buried us all in turn." Austin tells us that he was the symbol of Jimville's respectability, "although he was of a sect that held dancing among the cardinal sins." And so a respectful compromise was enacted: "The management took no chances on offending the minister; at 11:30 they tendered him the receipts of the evening in the chairman's hat, as a delicate intimation that the fair was closed. The company filed out of the front door and around the back. Then the dance began formally with no feelings hurt. These were the sort of courtesies, common enough in Jimville, that brought tears of delicate inner laughter."

As is commonly the case throughout literary natural history, a text is as much a window into the author's psyche as it is into the natural world upon which the narrative is focused. Although I had previously read biographical accounts of Austin's life, when I finally got around to reading Austin's autobiography, *Earth Horizon*, I learned a great deal about what went into the composition of *The Land of Little Rain*.

Before anything, it was interesting to note the change in Austin's writing from the perspective of the three decades that passed between the composition of *The Land of Little Rain* and *Earth Horizons*. It's easy to forget, when reading the earlier work, that it was written by a writer in her early thirties grinding out her first book. In her autobiography, she writes about some of the same events from the vantage of an author in her early sixties, and the difference is stunning, especially in terms of her feminism and her evolving social consciousness. But it's also of interest to note the challenges that learning the fundamentals of desert ecology posed. Referring to herself in the third person, she writes that "her trouble was that the country failed to explain itself. If it had a history, nobody could recount it. Its creatures had no known life except such as she could discover by unremitting vigilance of observation; its plants no names that her Middlewestern botany could supply."

We should not wonder that her approach to natural history was divergent from writers such as Thoreau and Burroughs, and we are aware that she was familiar with their work from a humorous mention of them she makes in *Earth Horizons*. In Book II: "The Thoughts of Youth are Long, Long Thoughts," Austin quoted restrictions her mother imposed upon her during her early teens: "You must not talk appreciatively about landscapes and flowers and the habits of little animals and birds to boys; they don't like it. If one of them took you walking, your interest should be in your companion, and not exceed a ladylike appreciation of the surroundings, in so far as the boy, as the author of the walk, might feel himself complimented by your appreciation of it. You must not quote; especially poetry and Thoreau. An occasional light reference to Burroughs was permissible, but not Thoreau."

Regardless of a dearth of field guides from which she could study the local ecology, Austin adopted a similar process of rigorous observation as Thoreau and Burroughs, moving beyond the basics of taxonomy into animal behavior and plant evolution. Where she goes beyond previous nature writing is in her emphasis on human relationships with the desert, and her empathy for the acquired wisdom of people close to the land, especially in terms of what she could learn from Indigenous peoples as well as Hispanic settlers. This empathy must have been sparked by the fact that a great deal of her knowledge of the desert landscape was gained by interactions with the people eking a living from an arid environment, not as she had learned botany previously in an academic setting.

In a chapter about Las Uvas, "The Little Town of the Grape Leaves," Austin's appreciation for popular culture goes on for seven pages, as is exemplified in the following paragraph:

At Las Uvas they keep up all the good customs brought out of Old Mexico or bred in a lotus-eating land; drink, and are merry and look out for something to eat afterward; have children, nine or ten to a family, have cock-fights, keep the siesta, smoke cigarettes and wait for the sun to go down. And always they dance; at dusk on the smooth adobe floors, afternoons under the trellises where the earth is damp and has a fruity smell. A betrothal, a wedding, or a christening, or the mere proximity of a guitar is sufficient occasion; and if the occasion lacks, send for the guitar and dance anyway.

As much as anything, in the Las Uvas chapter, Austin seems to delight that the town's culture is so accessible to her, everything from their process of sharing sustenance between families to their religious rituals and observations. This contrasts with Shoshone and Paiute culture, which Austin had to work harder to access, perhaps because she was dealing with Indigenous people who had already been subjugated and had been moved onto reservations.

While the quest to find meaning in nature is in no way unique to Austin's writing, her philosophical underpinnings are distinct from pastoral and transcendental approaches, especially in terms of valuing the wisdom of Native American culture. As she rebelled against the Methodist doctrine of nonconformity to the world, she also rejected Christian notions of the afterlife. Those beliefs were replaced by deeper appreciation of the human–nature relationship. Throughout *The Land of Little Rain*, Austin reflects that the more humanity adapts itself to the demands of the region in which it finds itself, the better it is not only for nature but also for humanity as well. In essence, she did not want her life to be a proving ground for admission into heaven but rather wanted it to be a process of adapting to the natural world.

Ultimately, Austin rejected human–nature boundaries that other writers of her time perceived as being fundamental. This is no doubt why her approach to natural history reflects a fluidity between nature and culture: she appreciated the diversity of human cultures in the same way she appreciated the biodiversity of desert flora, and she delighted when humans lived in harmony with their environment. Unfortunately, she didn't take this far in terms of developing an environmental ethic, but the basis for one was there, which is an important first step. This may be one of the reasons that scholars are currently more entranced with Austin's work, especially *The Land of Little Rain*, than they were half a century ago. In essence, we've been catching up to her, not only in terms of her feminism but also in terms of a progressive approach that decenters the human in nature.

Given this decentered approach, it makes sense that Austin showed no interest in preserving pristine, unscathed nature. Austin was on a different page than her contemporaries such as John Muir and John Burroughs, especially considering that her book was published during the presidency of Theodore Roosevelt. In an era when the dominant environmental discourse was one of wilderness preservation, Austin had other agendas, none of which was particularly political, all of which prized adaptation to the landscape.

The following passage demonstrates Austin's unique concern for wildlife, in this case a pair of nesting meadowlarks:

> There are hints to be had here of the way in which a land forces new habits on its dwellers. The quick increase of suns at the end of spring sometimes overtakes birds in their nesting and effects a reversal of the ordinary manner of incubation. It becomes necessary to keep eggs cool rather than warm. One hot, stifling spring in the Little Antelope I had occasion to pass and repass frequently the nest of a pair of meadowlarks, located unhappily in the shelter of a very slender weed. I never caught them sitting except near night, but at midday they stood, or drooped above it, half fainting with pitifully parted bills, between their treasure and the sun. Sometimes both of them together with wings spread and half lifted continued a spot of shade in a temperature that constrained me at last in a fellow feeling to spare them a bit of canvas for permanent shelter. There was a fence in that country shutting in a cattle range, and along its fifteen miles of posts one could be sure of finding a bird or two in every strip of shadow; sometimes the sparrow and the hawk, with wings trailed and beaks parted, drooping in the white truce of noon.

It would probably be inaccurate to view Austin's "sparing a bit of canvas for permanent shelter" as being a conservation measure. Her generosity, rather, was sparked by what she calls "fellow feeling," a sense of interspecies community. Empathy was involved here for fellow creatures at a time when both she and the meadowlarks were suffering the stifling temperature. It's also interesting to note that the fence posts that provide shade for sparrow and hawk are not viewed by Austin as an intrusion on the landscape, as they might have been by other nature writers, both contemporaries and those writing after her time. The birds had learned to utilize human structures just as humans had learned to make glue for arrow points from creosote resin. In Austin's view, it's all good as long as creatures learn to survive in the landscapes in which they find themselves. The same rules apply to humans, meadowlarks and plants: the good is found in the ability to adapt.

A pattern emerges as regards both Austin's attention and affection. Her admiration is not reserved for the most charismatic individuals or species. Rather, it goes to those creatures who thrive in a challenging environment and do so in a way that exemplifies what Austin would consider a spiritual resolve. This is perhaps why she wrote a chapter on scavengers rather than charismatic megafauna, such as bighorn sheep, bears, or other predators. Indeed, in the final paragraph of "The Scavengers," she wrote:

> Man is a great blunderer going about the woods, and there is no other except the bear makes so much noise. Being so well warned beforehand, it is a very stupid animal, or a very bold one, that cannot keep safely hid. The cunningest hunter is hunted in turn, and what he leaves of his kill is meat for some other. That is the economy of nature, but with it all there is not sufficient account of the works of man. There is no scavenger that eats tin cans, and no wild thing leaves a like disfigurement on the forest floor.

In other words, we could learn a thing or two from the scavengers and other life-forms that were considered lowly at the turn of the nineteenth century, beginning with the fact that we should clean up after ourselves. Note however, in that final sentence, that Austin still can be mired in conventional binaries: "No wild thing" litters the forest floor with tin cans.

Austin clearly understands that she is not conforming to the mold of a Western writer. She criticizes her contemporaries, scolding, "Western writers have not sensed it yet; they smack the savor of lawlessness too much upon their tongues, but you have these [citizens of Jimville] to witness it is not mean-spiritedness." And that is ultimately the strength of her reportage: she was there as a witness, whether in the encampments of the Paiute, the far mesas of Shoshone Land, a rough-and-tumble miners camp, a village of Mexican transplants, Death Valley, or the high Sierras.

If there is an ethic to be found in *The Land of Little Rain*, it is one of being observant. Whether you're a plant, a coyote, or a human being, the desert will dictate how to thrive within it, but it can only do that if you're able to hear the dictation. One must perceive the landscape with new eyes, seeing beyond the old conventions. Just as one of the boundaries she blurs is the gap between nature and culture, she also obscures the usual demarcations between wilderness and civilization, the wild and the domestic, and male and female.

While Austin's feminism isn't as well defined in *The Land of Little Rains* as it would be in her later writing, it is nascent. She is not inclined to sit safely inside the stagecoach when the view is better up beside the driver. She makes keen observations, here and there, about womanly behavior, for example, "In our kind of society, when a woman ceases to alter the fashion of her hair, you guess that she has passed the crisis of her experience. If she goes on crimping and uncrimping with the changing mode, it is safe to suppose she has never come up against anything too big for her." More to the point, she does not allow her gender to constrain her investigations, confident that the truth behind her observations will excuse any lines of propriety she had to transgress in order to gain her viewpoints.

In the final section of her autobiography, Austin reflected on her career as a writer and the decisions she made as to where she should devote her attention. There was never to be another book of similar scope to *The Land of Little Rain*, despite a clamor for a follow-up, both from her readership and her publishers. Looking back, the mature Mary Austin replied truthfully: "I recall that people used to fret at me because I would not do another 'Land of the Little Rain.' I couldn't, of course, I had used up all I had on the first one. I should have had to find another country like that, and pay out ten thousand dollars to live in it ten or twelve years. I wrote what I lived, what I had observed and understood. Then I stopped."

Despite her claim that the desert acquired a life-long hold of its inhabitants, Austin was not to stay put in the land of little rain. Four years after the publication of her masterwork, she would move on to the writer colony of Carmel-by-the-Sea, and thereafter would inhabit the publishing world of New York City, and then finally move to the artist conclave of Santa Fe, always more a pioneer than a settler. She died there in August of 1934, the same month that Adolf Hitler was proclaimed *Führer* of Nazi Germany.

Ways of Nature by John Burroughs (1905)

Nature reaches her ends by devious paths; she loiters, she meanders, she plays by the way; she surely "arrives," but it is always in a blind, hesitating, experimental kind of fashion. —FROM THE CHAPTER, "DEVIOUS PATHS"

The Victorian Age officially began in 1837, the year that Queen Victoria ascended to her throne. This was the year when Chicago and Houston were both incorporated, the latter becoming a city within the Independent Republic of Texas. Also in 1837, Samuel Morse filed a patent for the telegraph; the Seminoles attacked Fort Foster in Florida; Nathaniel Hawthorn published the first volume of his short-story collection, *Twice-Told Tales*; Michigan became the twenty-sixth state in the union; and Henry David Thoreau was selected to make one of the commencement speeches during his graduation from Harvard College. The gunslinger Wild Bill Hickok and the writer John Burroughs were both born in 1837.

Burroughs life began on a family farm in the Catskill Mountains near Roxbury, New York. The year he was born only 18 percent of the inhabitants of New York state lived in cities. By the time he died, in 1921, more than 75 percent of New Yorkers would be urbanized. This transition from rural to urban lifestyles came at a tremendous emotional cost, especially to those who had been born on farms but now worked in urban factories. The things these displaced people missed the most were the animals with which they'd formerly lived, and by the time Burroughs began to establish himself as a writer, the hottest ticket in the publishing world was for stories about animals.

Burroughs had a few lucky breaks right off the bat. His 1860 essay, "Expressions," was picked up by an emerging periodical, *The Atlantic*, and he would go on to publish more than four hundred essays in popular magazines of the time.* His other major break came 1863, where an opening as a clerk in the Currency Bureau prompted a move to Washington, DC, where he befriended Walt Whitman. The great poet and essayist ultimately convinced Burroughs that he should develop a literature about nature that integrated precise observation with poetic expression. Doing so, Burroughs not only became America's most popular nature writer but also its most popular writer of any genre, his popularity exceeding that of his mentor.

Most of the twenty-three volumes of books that Burroughs authored were collections of his previously published essays. The first of these, *Wake-Robin*, published in 1871, was so successful that he was able to return home to the Catskill Mountains and work full-time as a writer. Noting his success, a number of other writers started to write about wild animals, but the problem was that many of them had little knowledge of natural history and ended up fabricating many of the facts they wrote about. The point came, near the turn of the century, that the American reading public was being fed a steady stream of nonsense about such things as snakes who would form a hoop by biting their tail and then roll away from adversaries, or perhaps a fictional account of a mix-breed sled dog who escapes to the Alaskan wild and becomes the alpha breeder in a pack of wolves.† These works were sentimental and presented a storybook view of nature and animal behavior. The American public gobbled it all up.

In 1905, Burroughs, aware that his own writing had been overly sentimental in bits and snatches, published his sixteenth book, *Ways of Nature*, a collection of essays that marked a turning point in his career. The introduction contained a gentle critique of "the new school of nature writers or natural history romancers that has lately arisen, and that reads into the birds and animals almost the entire human psychology." The issue, as he saw it, was animal intelligence, and he complained that

---

* Ultimately forty of Burroughs's essays were published in *The Atlantic*, including "A Critical Glance into Thoreau," which came out in the June 1919 issue. Burroughs's thesis was that the natural history in Thoreau's books was of a secondary nature to his work as a "critic of life." Burroughs claimed that "his science is only the handmaid of his ethics; his wood-lore is the foil of his moral and intellectual teachings." As such, "he was, first and last, a moral force speaking in the terms of a literary naturalist."

† Buck, the animal hero in Jack London's *Call of the Wild*, was a cross between a Saint Bernard and Scottish Shepherd. Burroughs was not a fan of London's fiction.

some authors "pervert natural history and give false impressions of the intelligence of our animals, catering to a taste that prefers the fanciful to the true and the real." He complained further than a "great army of readers prefer this sugar-coated natural history to the real thing."

Burroughs's solution, as he saw it, was that the real nature lover would prefer "unadulterated, unsweetened observations of the natural world." He claimed that human inventions of animal behaviors and traits could never be as interesting as true natural history based on observations, which would have scientific value. He laid out his argument with clear examples of animal intelligence being over-characterized and with certain faith that his devoted readers would rise above the romanticized literature that was flooding the market.

The first essay in the collection, "Bird Song," seems indeed to be addressed to a sophisticated audience who would be able to identify common birds such as song sparrows, meadowlarks, purple finches, and woodcocks. Before describing any of their songs, he rejects poetic notions equating birdsong with music, by which he seems to mean human music, and makes the case that recognizing and appreciating birdsong requires a fair amount of skill development. He argues that since birdsong is part of nature, that becoming attuned to it requires effort, claiming that "the ear that hears them must be half creative." He also makes the point that immersion in the outdoors adds to the appreciation of birdsong. "A stranger would probably recognize melody and a wild woodsy quality in the flutings of the veery thrush; but how much more they would mean to him after he had spent many successive Junes threading our northern trout-streams and encamping on their banks!" Despite this assertion, he seems to want to disassociate himself from ecstatic descriptions of the birdsong.

Eager to dispel mistaken observations of natural history, in the following essay, "Nature with Closed Doors," Burroughs catalogues how even academics and scientists sometimes get things wrong. Providing specific examples, he writes, "I saw it stated the other day, in a paper read before some scientific body, that the wood frogs retreat two feet into the ground beyond the reach of frost." He insists that there have been two instances where he has found a wood frog in December protected by a covering of less than two inches of leaves and moss, and he theorizes that the snow itself provides most of the frog's thermal protection. Likewise, he notes, "I have seen it stated in a rhetorical flight of some writer that the new buds crowd the old leaves off." He insists that this is not true as a rule, observing that the new bud is formed in the axial of the old leaf before it falls off the tree. He also reports that a correspondent, "writing to me from one of the colleges," inaccurately suggested that spring actually begins in December because the annual cycle of vegetable life seems to begin then. The pattern in these three misinterpretations of natural history is clear: the first mistake comes from a paper "read before some scientific body"; the second is stated in "a rhetorical flight by some writer"; and the third is from a correspondent "from one of the colleges." Burroughs, ever the gentleman, avoids embarrassing these experts by naming them in print, but the point seems to be that, since scientists, published writers, and academics can get natural history wrong, the reader must always take a critical stance. There also seems to be a hint of pride in Burroughs's personal observations, going unsaid that the true naturalist is the one who abandons comfort and makes observations out in the winter cold, especially when wood frogs are involved.

The next essay, "The Wit of a Duck," serves to demonstrate a homing instinct that birds have that humans do not. In it, Burroughs's son borrows a mallard drake from a neighbor to breed it to his two hens and brings it home in a bag. We must assume that this was a domestic mallard, *Anas platyrhynchos domesticus*, because, as we will discover during the narrative, it cannot fly. The duck is not happy at the Burroughs's farm, especially when kept in the barn with its potential mates. After a few days, Burroughs mercifully decided that duck should return home and said to his son, "If that drake is really bound to go home, he shall have an opportunity to make the trial, and I will go with him to see that he has fair play." So Burroughs followed the duck, both of them walking, two miles back to its home, noting that it only became confused a couple of times, once needing Burroughs's help to get over a wall.

The ending of this narrative is strange because it runs counter to Burroughs's project of not ascribing human emotion to animals. The final paragraph of the essay reads, "I followed close. Into the house yard he rushed with uplifted wings, and fell down almost exhausted by the side of his mate. A half hour later the two were nipping the grass together in the pasture, and he, I have no doubt, was eagerly telling her the story of his adventures." Here the author ends a tale as was typical of animal stories at the turn of the century, supplying a humorous resolution by imagining the animal to behave the way a human might after the long journey to be reunited with a mate. It's as if Burroughs could not resist juicing up that final sentence in a story that otherwise demonstrated that his theories were backed up by trustworthy observations afield.

Burroughs is making a complex, extended argument here, with each essay containing a major point to advance the book's line of reasoning. This argument becomes obvious not only in the essays that are selected for inclusion in the book but also in the order in which they are presented. The next essay, "Factors in Animal Life," contains a long sentence that exemplifies a critique of sentimentalism that becomes central to Burroughs's argument:

> When hospitals are founded for sick or homeless cats and dogs, when all forms of vivisection are cried down, when the animals are humanized and books are written to show that the wild creatures have schools and kindergartens, and that their young are instructed and disciplined in quite the human way by their fond parents; when we want to believe that reason and not instinct guides them, that they are quite up in some of the simpler arts of surgery, mending or amputating their own broken limbs and salving their wounds,—when, I say, our attitude toward the natural life about us and our feeling for it have reached the stage implied by these things, then has sentiment degenerated into sentimentalism, and our appreciation of nature lost its firm edge.

Before analyzing that sentence, some historical background: The first small animal hospitals in New York were being founded during the 1880s, and the idea of providing medical care for cats and dogs was controversial, with many Americans considering such care an extravagance. Prior to then, veterinary medicine was mostly confined to large animals, for the most part farm animals. The American Anti-Vivisection Society was formed in Philadelphia in 1883 with the expressed goal of regulating scientific experimentation on animals. It was modeled on similar organizations that had sprung up in Great Britain, where a cruelty-to-animals act had been passed in 1867. Burroughs disagrees with the sentimentality behind both movements.

Returning to our close reading of the above-quoted sentence. Although Burroughs doesn't mention the book by title or the author's name, most of his readers would have recognized the book about animal schools and kindergartens as *School of the Woods: Some Life Studies of Animal Instincts and Animal Training*, by the Reverend William J. Long, a Congregationalist minister, published in 1902. It was a popular book in its day.

Long's thesis, found in the preface, was bound to infuriate Burroughs. He wrote: "That animal education is like our own, and so depends chiefly upon teaching, may possibly be a new suggestion in the field of natural history. Most people think that the life of a wild animal is governed wholly by instinct. They are of the same class who hold that the character of a child is predetermined by heredity."

Here is a sample paragraph from one of Long's chapters, "A School for Little Fishermen," about an osprey mother—the author refers to this species as "fish-hawks,"—teaching two fledglings how to fish:

> It is clear now to even my eyes that there is a vast difference in the characters of young fishhawks. The first was eager, headstrong, impatient; the second is calmer, stronger, more obedient. He watches the mother; he heeds her signals. Five minutes later he makes a clean, beautiful swoop and comes up with his fish. The mother whistles her praise as she drops beside him. My eyes follow them as, gossiping like two old cronies, they wing their slow way over the dancing whitecaps and climb the slanting tree-tops to the nest.

It's easy to see why this book was included in nearly every school library in the country. There is a moral here, that the obedient child who heeds his mother's instructions will ultimately win the prize as well as earn his mother's praise. It is the headstrong child's fault when he goes to bed hungry. Of course, the truth of the matter is that osprey do not have an articulate language capable of instructing the young on technique,* and osprey fledglings mostly learn to fish via trial and error. It's also unlikely that anyone who has witnessed an osprey hunt firsthand would describe it as "a clean, beautiful swoop" because they usually plunge completely underwater, and the process of emerging with the fish involves considerable strain, especially before the osprey gains enough altitude to shake the water from its feathers, similar to how dogs shake off water after emerging from a swim.

What follows is a chapter on animal communication where Burroughs makes the point that European writers on natural history, including Darwin, Wallace, Brehm, Büchner, and the Müllers no longer subscribe to the opinion that animals consciously train and educate their young. He does allow, however, that some learning takes place via instinctive play. For Burroughs, teaching implies reflection and judgment as well as implying "a thought of, and solicitude for, the future." He points out, however, that what animals lack in wit they make up in caution, adding that animals are afraid on general principle, wary of anything new and strange.

Controversies about animal cognition will not resolve fully for at least another century; indeed, there are discoveries still being made that indicate that animals

---

* Earlier in the story Long had described the mother's instructions as a series of pips, chirps, and whistles. While osprey indeed chirp, they tend to communicate meaning, especially alarm, by modulating the intensity of those chirps.

are capable of higher-level thinking than we previously thought. The point here is more about the practice of natural history than animal psychology. Burroughs was advocating for a discipline based on direct, critical observation, not imagination and certainly not fantasy.

Throughout his career, Burroughs would write about the art of seeing, and this writing was not merely prescriptive—he would also provide examples of how his own observations led to conclusions. An example of this occurs in the following chapter, "Devious Paths," where he describes an evening when, while sitting on his porch, he had "convincing proof" that song competitions sometimes took place among birds. In this case, it was two wood thrushes who kept together at the top of a tree snag and alternated singing. He wrote, "They sang and sang with unwearied spirit and persistence, now and then changing position or facing in another direction, but keeping within a few feet of each other. The rivalry became so obvious and was so interesting that I finally made it a point not to take my eyes from the singers." This went on for more than half an hour until darkness descended, and Burroughs concluded that they were competing for a mate. At the end of it, he wrote, "Had the birds been birds of brilliant plumage, the rivalry would probably have taken the form of strutting and showing off their bright colors and ornaments."

Burroughs is clearly attempting to incorporate the latest discoveries from science, especially those of Charles Darwin, into his reflections. In that same chapter, he reflects, "The law of variation is everywhere operative—less so now, no doubt, than in the earlier history of organic life on the globe. Yet Nature is still experimenting in her blind way, and hits upon many curious differences and departures. But I suppose if the race of man were exterminated, man would never arise again. I doubt if the law of evolution could ever again produce him, or any other species of animal."

Despite its immense popularity during Burroughs's lifetime, the writing has not stood the test of time and is seldom read these days beyond scholars of literary natural history. A review of his eighth chapter, "Do Animals Think and Reflect?" from a contemporary perspective shows why, at least partially. The science on animal cognition has moved far beyond his early twentieth-century speculation and indeed has proved many of his assertions wrong. Burroughs, for example, claims that crows cannot possibly utilize tools, and yet today, if I get on Google Scholar and search under "tool use by crows," I will uncover links to hundreds of scientific studies proving him wrong. But I feel that to look for scientific cohesion in Burroughs's writing is to look past his major contribution, which was to insist on standards of rigor and accuracy in literary natural history. Even at the risk of his own authorial popularity, for *Ways of Nature* is less entertaining than much of his prior work, he was willing to put aside his vibrant storytelling throughout much of the book in order to provide a corrective for the nature writing of his time. In essence, he was propounding an argument targeted as much to other nature writers as it was to the reading public.

It should be noted that *Ways of Nature* was not his first attempt to provide this corrective. Two years earlier, he had published an article, "Real and Sham Nature Writing" in the *Atlantic Monthly*. In that article, he had specifically targeted the work of three popular authors, William Long, Ernest Thompson Seaton, and Jack London, and the article provoked a great deal of controversy, one that would rage for the better part of a decade. This controversy engaged the national interest to the point that President Theodore Roosevelt ultimately got involved, siding with Burroughs and publishing his own article, "Nature Fakers," in a 1907 issue of *Everybody's Magazine*. Roosevelt went so far as to insist that Long's books be removed from the shelves of school libraries.*

Even prior to the "Real and Sham Nature Writing" article, Burroughs had been advocating accuracy in literary natural history. As far back as in the introduction to his first collection of essays he wrote that "the literary naturalist does not take liberties with facts; facts are the flora upon which he lives. The more and the fresher the facts the better."

What Burroughs was campaigning for here went beyond demanding that literary natural history, as a nonfiction genre, not contain fiction. He insisted further that nature writing should be based on direct observation in the field. His strongest critique was that some of his contemporaries' major sources of outdoor data was what they read in sporting magazines, such as *Field and Stream*, which was founded the year his first book was published.

Burroughs certainly had his critics, and he acknowledges this in the book's tenth chapter, "A Pinch of Salt." He writes: "One of my critics says, apropos of certain recent strictures of mine upon some current nature writers, that I discredit whatever I have not myself seen; that I belong to that class of observers 'whose view-point is narrowed to the limit of their own personal experience.'" He insists, to the contrary, that a certain amount of trust has to be placed in natural history,

---

* An excellent history of this controversy can be found in Ralph H. Lutts, *Nature Fakers: Wildlife, Science and Sentiment* (Charlottesville: University of Virginia Press, 2001).

just as is necessary in all history. But he points out that in matters of belief it is apparent that the scientific method is "not of equal favor with all minds. Some persons believe what they can or must, others what they would. One person agrees with his reason and experience, another what is agreeable to his or her fantasy."

This controversy has echoes even today among nature writers. Many contemporary authors, and I included myself among this group, combine personal history with natural history in a way that would not be characteristic of pure science writing, which tends to be more reportorial to the extent that any element of memoir is expunged. For most of us, regardless, it is important to the integrity of our work that the natural history is informed by science, not only the science of evolution and ecology but also conservation science. This does not require us to become scientists in the sense in that we don't have to collect and analyze data according to a scientific method. However, this does require, at least for me, spending an appropriate amount of time in the field, not only observing natural history skillfully but also keeping contemporaneous field notes. This, I feel, is John Burroughs's legacy.

As Burroughs viewed it, the difficulty is that it's so hard to set standards of what is reasonable in terms of natural history. Take this passage for example:

> Or if you tell me that you have seen an old doe with horns, or a hen with spurs, or a male bird incubating and singing on the nest, unusual as the last occurrence is, I shall not dispute you. I will concede that you may have seen a white crow or a white blackbird or a white robin, or a black chipmunk or a black red squirrel, and many other departures from the usual in animal life; but I cannot share the conviction of the man who told me he had seen a red squirrel curing rye before storing it up in its den, or of the writer who believes the fox will ride upon the back of a sheep to escape the hound, or of another writer that he has seen the blue heron chumming for fish.

Well, I have witnessed male birds incubating eggs, and peer-reviewed ornithology journals are rife with observations of herons employing bait in their fishing, including the black-crowned night heron (*Nyticorax nyticorax*), the green heron (*Bulorides virescens*), the striated heron (*Butorides striatus*); the great egret (*Ardea alba*), and the great blue heron (*Ardea herodias*). Having made this point, I stand with Burroughs in doubting any tale of a fox riding upon the back of a sheep to escape the hound. Call me a skeptic.

Having listed in his tenth chapter dozens of written accounts of animal behavior that he flat-out rejects, in the eleventh chapter, "The Literary Treatment of Nature," Burroughs finally deals with the difference between literary and scientific treatments of nature. He begins with the acknowledgment, "The literary treatment of natural history themes is, of course, quite different from the scientific treatment, and should be so." He asserts that literature provides truth in such ways as to touch the reader's emotions, and "to satisfy the enjoyment we have in the living reality." In comparing the literary artist to "his scientific brother," he points out that the artist's method is synthetic rather than analytic. By this statement, he means that a process of synthesizing takes place where the nature writer is communicating truths arrived at in the field and the woods rather than the laboratory. Further, he points out that what he calls "the essay-naturalist" observes and admires while the scientific naturalist collects, the former enlisting your sympathies and arousing your enthusiasm, the latter adding to your store of knowledge.

If there is a manifesto in this section, it is deeply personal. Note the unifying way that Burroughs speaks collectively in the following passage, and yet where he shifts from plural to singular first-person pronouns.

> We like to see ourselves in the nature around us. We want in some way to translate these facts and laws of outward nature into our own experiences; to relate our observations of bird or beast to our own lives. Unless they beget some human emotion in me,—the emotion of the beautiful, the sublime,—or appeal to my sense of the fit, the permanent,—unless what you learn in the fields and the woods corresponds in some way with what I know of my fellows, I shall not long be deeply interested in it. I do not want the animals humanized in any other sense.

Burroughs makes one further point in this chapter that many of today's nature writers might find troubling, stating that "strictly speaking there is not much in natural history that needs interpreting." Later, he clarifies that natural history is not a cryptograph to be deciphered, but rather is a series of facts and incidents to be observed and recorded. A few authors covered later in this study might take issue with such an assertion, especially those who view natural history through the lens of cultural interpretation as well as through science.

Burroughs doesn't claim to have all the answers. In the book's penultimate chapter, "Reading the Book of Nature," he describes a widespread, severe drought during the spring of 1903. When the rains finally came in late June, he noted something unusual, that the marshes around him were again resounding with the voices of spring peepers.* Burroughs is not entirely sure why this happened. He is clear on the fact of what happened, but uncertain as to the interpretation. Did the drought cause them to remain in the marshes where they could at least find some moisture? Did the originally depart for their life in the woods, only to return once it rained to give breeding a second attempt? After considering such options, he confesses that he doesn't know. He proposes the most rational possibility he could conjure, that they hibernated in the marshes during the dry months of spring, but he doesn't want to base natural history on such conjecture.†

Burroughs ends the chapter with an admonition that for better or worse seems to have become his personal credo: "The power to see straight is the rarest of gifts; to see no more and no less than is actually before you; to be able to detach yourself and see the thing as it actually is, uncolored or unmodified by your own sentiments or prepossessions. In short, to see with your reason as well as with your perceptions, that is to be an observer and to read the book of nature aright."

In the end, a flaw in Burroughs approach may be the extent to which he hopes to distinguish between human and nonhuman intelligence among animals. In the final chapter of the book, "Gathered by the Way," he makes a final argument for the case that the major difference between humans and other animals is instinct, which he sees as a different kind of intelligence than humans possess. However, he feels that animal intelligence is a limiting factor. Because animals do not learn from instruction or experience, as Burroughs sees it, they do not progress in knowledge over the period of their lifetimes. This contrasts with human intelligence, which he feels is "almost limitless." He continues, "A man is an animal born again into a higher spiritual plane. He has lost or shed many of his animal instincts in the process, but he has gained the capacity for great and wonderful improvement." Burroughs here subscribes to a dualism that pits instinct against reason, and in that

---

* Burroughs uses the genus name "Hyla," which is no longer in use. Today, spring peepers, a small chorus frog, common in the eastern United States and Canada, are described as *Pseudacris crucifer*.

† Recent studies have discovered that during times of drought, spring peepers will use caves as a refuge because the higher relative humidity contributes to their survival. See especially: J. Prather and J. Briggler, "Use of Small Caves by Anurans during a Drought Period in the Arkansas Ozarks," *Journal of Herpetology* 35, no. 4 (2001): 675–78. Although this study was conducted in the Ozark mountains, the Catskills contain caves that could have served a similar purpose.

way underestimates the wit of the animal kingdom, especially among longer-lived animals who learn a great deal over the course of a lifetime.

We must remember that Burroughs was a man of his time, a time when evolutionary theory was just coming to the fore. Although he embraced Darwin, Burroughs missed some fundamental implications of Darwin's system, especially when it came to animal behavior. That said, he played a vital role in bringing literary natural history back in line with science.

Because he was so prolific, the whole of Burroughs's influence cannot be based on any single book he wrote. *Ways of Nature*, for example, does not really include environmental thought. However, Burroughs went to considerable length in other collections to speak on behalf of conservation, especially that of birds. At the end of one essay, "Bird Enemies," after going through all the problems that nesting birds encounter, from snakes to mammals to other birds, he ends the essay decrying the depredations of egg collectors, even those who consider their collections as part of science.* This essay contains some of the strongest language I've seen come from Burroughs's pen, even to the extent of name-calling, referring to those who make a business of collecting eggs and bird specimens "bird-highwaymen." At the end of a long harangue, Burroughs concludes that professional nest-robbers "should be put down, either by legislation or with dogs and shot-guns." Burroughs then turns his attention to milliners, who he estimated caused the deaths of hundreds of thousands of birds each year by featuring feathers and indeed whole skins on women's hats, adding, "It is a barbarous taste that craves this kind of ornamentation."

Despite delivering such harsh criticism, Burroughs was generally regarded as a personable and upbeat writer. Henry James once wrote of him that "Mr. Burroughs is a sort of reduced, but also more humorous, more available, more sociable Thoreau."† This critique sat heavy on Burroughs's mind, and he ultimately wrote in his journal of February 26, 1878:

> I really see very little of Thoreau in myself. There is a whiff of him now and then, in a few of my pieces . . . I know his quality is very penetrating and contagious; reading him is like eating onions, one must look out

---

* This essay appeared in the book, *Birds and Bees, Sharp Eyes, and Other Papers*, published in 1887.

† Frank Bergon, *A Sharp Outlook: Selected Natural History Essays of John Burroughs* (Washington, DC: Smithsonian Institution Press, 1987), 24.

or the flavor will reach his own page. But my current is as strong in my own channel as T's in his. He is as liable to catch it of me as I am of him. Thoreau preaches and teaches always. I never preach or teach. I simply see and describe; I must have a pure result.

Burroughs ended *Ways of Nature* with a poem, as was not uncharacteristic of nature writing in Victorian times. An ode to the common crow, it provided a light flourish to what had otherwise been an intense book, its final four lines being particularly droll:

> *May I never cease to meet thee,*
> *May I never have to eat thee.*
> *And mayest thou never have to fare so*
> *That thou playest the part of scarecrow.*

A Sand County Almanac: And Sketches Here and There by Aldo Leopold (1949)

That land is a community is the basic concept of ecology, but that land is to be loved and respected is an extension of ethics. —FROM THE FOREWORD TO *A SAND COUNTY ALMANAC*

In 1887, Buffalo Bill's Wild West Show opened in London to celebrate the Golden Jubilee of Queen Victoria, the Dawes Act stripped over ninety million acres of reservation land from Native Americans, and Notre Dame lost its inaugural football game, 8–0, to Michigan. The cornerstone of Stanford University was laid. Groundhog Day was celebrated for the first time. Arthur Conan Doyle published the first Sherlock Holmes mystery that year, *A Study in Scarlet*, and Aldo Leopold was born in Burlington, Iowa.

Leopold turned thirteen when Yale University opened its Forest School, a pioneering endeavor to train foresters. Already an avid hunter and birder, Leopold hoped to become a forester, and his parents sent him to a preparatory college in New Jersey to improve his chances of admission to Yale. After a year studying there, he was accepted to Yale, but the Forestry School only offered graduate-level courses so Leopold enrolled in the Sheffield Scientific School in New Haven, Connecticut, to build an undergraduate foundation for forestry. From there, he went directly into the Forest School and was able to graduate from it in 1909 at the age of twenty-one.

In numerous ways, Leopold was in the right place at the right time. The United States Forest Service had been established in 1905 and provided tremendous opportunities for those knowledgeable about forestry, especially those willing to travel westward. Leopold was assigned to the Forest Service's District Three, which managed the Arizona and New Mexico territories. This was three years before the two territories would be granted statehood. His first assignment, as a forest assistant, was in the Apache National Forest in Arizona. Three years later, he transferred to the Carson National Forest in New Mexico as deputy supervisor, and, in the following year, 1911, he was promoted to supervisor. He would remain there until 1924. During that time, he developed the first comprehensive management plan for the Grand Canyon, which was established as a national park in 1919, he wrote the *Game and Fish Handbook* for the US Forest Service, and he proposed the Gila Wilderness Area, which was the world's first designated wilderness area.

In 1933, Leopold was appointed professor of game management at the University of Wisconsin, becoming the first professor of wildlife management in all of higher education. This was in the same year that his seminal book, *Game Management*, was published. The book revolutionized wildlife management by integrating concepts of food chains, ecology, and population dynamics into habitat protection. Shortly thereafter, he helped co-found the Wilderness Society, a conservation organization dedicated to expanding wilderness protection throughout the nation.*

If *Game Management* read like a textbook, *A Sand County Almanac: And Sketches Here and There* reads like an insider's guide to the biotic community. While it is thoroughly informed by science, it is rich with figurative expression. For example, in describing the lifespan of the needles of coniferous trees, Leopold writes, "Pines have earned the reputation of being 'evergreen' by the same device that governments use to achieve the appearance of perpetuity: overlapping terms of office. By taking on new needles on the new growth of each year, and discarding old needles at longer intervals, they have led the casual onlooker to believe that needles remain forever green."

Leopold's critique throughout the book is not focused on government, however, so much as it is aimed at modernity. Early on in the book's foreword, Leopold writes, "For us of the minority, the opportunity to see geese is more important than television, and the chance to find a pasque-flower is a right as inalienable as free speech." Over the course of the next few paragraphs, Leopold sets himself up an

---

* Of the seven original founders of the society, two would be honored by having a wilderness area named in their memory: Bob Marshall and Aldo Leopold.

outlier, especially where he states, "We of the minority see the law of diminishing returns in progress, our opponents do not." The shift here is subtle: where Thoreau critiqued society through the lens of economy, Leopold critiques economics through the lens of community. This thesis is set out clearly by the end of the foreword: "Conservation is getting nowhere because it is incompatible with our Abrahamic concept of land. We abuse land because we regard it as a commodity belonging to us. When we see land as a community to which we belong, we may begin to use it with love and respect."

There, ultimately, is the entire book in a nutshell: it's about community, a biotic community to which we belong, and toward which we have ethical responsibilities. The implications of this, to Leopold, are wide-ranging, as are the consequences for the biosphere.

Leopold develops the book in three distinct movements, and this is part of its genius. The first part is the almanac itself, arranged seasonally, month by month, set in "The Shack," a refuge where his family takes weekend respites from modernity. The second, "Episodes Here and There," is arranged regionally and episodically and narrates how Leopold became aware of conservation issues, "gradually and sometimes painfully." The third, which Leopold calls "The Upshot," proposes his famous land ethic. Toward the end of the foreword, Leopold warns that "only the very sympathetic reader will wish to wrestle with the philosophical questions of Part III. I suppose it may be said that these essays tell the company how it may get back in step." Rather than merely suggesting conservation measures, he ultimately propose a shift in values.

While much of the book will end up in philosophical reflection, its structure is essentially narrative. This gives the work a literary feel and is probably the trick that works the book's magic. Rather than engaging us the way a professor instructs students, Leopold emerges as a master storyteller, relating episodes in a heartfelt, down-to-earth way. A trust is built between author and reader where we become part of the minority who understand why and how things must change. And we gradually understand that while many of *A Sand County Almanac*'s tales comprise a man's memoir, the overarching narrative is more about the land as this man experienced it.

The first almanac essay, titled "January Thaw," is short and simple. It narrates the trail of a hibernating skunk who awakens during a thaw and "uncurls himself and ventures forth to prowl the wet world, dragging his belly in the snow." The narrator follows the skunk's trail, "curious to deduce his state of mind and appetite, and destination if any." In the process of doing this, the narrator startles a meadow mouse that has just crossed the skunk's trail. The speculation is made that the meadow mouse is aggrieved by the thaw because it exposed the snow tunnels that kept the mouse safe prior to the thaw. "To the mouse," we are told, "snow means freedom from want and fear."

The scene shifts to a rough-legged hawk, sailing over the meadow, who stops, "hovers like a kingfisher, and then drops like a feathered bomb into the marsh." The hawk has captured a mouse, and we learn that it has come down from the Arctic in the hope of thaws, "for to him a thaw means freedom from want and fear." We resume our tracking of the skunk at this point, entering the woods and crossing a glade where a rabbit has packed down the snow. We come across a bloody spot, "encircled by a wide-sweeping arc of owl's wings." After reflecting on the lesson the rabbit was taught, we follow the skunk track again, until it finally enters a pile of driftwood and doesn't emerge. The narration concludes, "I hear the tinkle of dripping water among the logs, and I fancy the skunk hears it too. I turn homeward, still wondering."

This tale of a simple outing during a January thaw tells us a great deal about its author. First of all, he is an attentive naturalist, capable of distinguishing the tracks of small mammals from each other. He readily identifies a rough-legged hawk and is aware of both its migratory history and hunting methodology. He knows that the wing-pattern in the snow was made by a different raptor entirely. All this knowledge he brings to the field, and yet his winter walk leaves him still wondering. Readers such as me are left with the feeling that we'd have loved to accompany this naturalist on a winter walk, and indeed we have.

The next entry into the almanac, "Good Oak," begins with the admonition, "There are two spiritual dangers in not owning a farm. One is the danger of supposing that breakfast comes from the grocery, and the other that heat comes from the furnace." In 1937, Leopold searched for land where he could stage family hunting trips. The farm he found, near the Wisconsin River, was by any description a windswept, worn-out piece of land, available for eight dollars an acre. The Leopold family—mom, dad, and five kids—took it on as a project and would ultimately plant 40,000 trees on it, the majority of which died at first due to drought conditions. They transformed the old chicken coup into a summer retreat they affectionately called "The Shack," which is now a national historic landmark. This place engendered *A Sand County Almanac*, its essays being crafted over an eleven-year period.

Leopold only mentions The Shack twice in the book. The foreword references it as a weekend refuge for his family from "too much modernity," adding, "On this sand farm in Wisconsin, first worn out and then abandoned by our bigger-and-better society, we try to rebuild, with shovel and axe, what we are losing elsewhere. It is here that we seek—and still find—our meat from God." In the second mention we learn, in passing, that the building is heated by firewood. Secondary sources reveal the structure to have originally been a twelve-by-eighteen-foot chicken coop onto which the Leopold family added a ten-by-twelve-foot bunkhouse, on which they first laid a clay floor with a hand-built fireplace and chimney. Over the years, they whitewashed the interior, added a wooden floor, and added chinking and battens to the vertical barnwood cladding. Most of the wood used in the shack's expansion was driftwood claimed from the nearby river, which provided an economical way to build a vacation home during the Great Depression.

As compelling as the almanac section of the book may be, these days the book is known for its later essays and for the environmental thought contained within them, much of which is original with its author. Part II is named, simply, "Sketches Here and There," and is a compendium of place-based essays that illustrate environmental degradation that was common during the 1930s. Here Leopold makes a shift from nature observation, which is what his publisher wanted, toward exposition about conservation issues, which is what the author insisted on writing about. In essence, he wanted to transcend natural history so that ecology would become a primary concern. It is for this reason that it took Leopold the better part of a decade—eight years of constant revisions—to get the book close to publishable form. The book had started off as a project with the publisher Knopf, but they explicitly wanted description of nature, such as what is contained in the first section of the book. At the same time, Leopold's first choice for a title of the manuscript was *Conservation Ecology*, which at one point morphed into *Land Ecology*. Knopf, incidentally, pulled out of the project after three years of reviewing Leopold's manuscripts and urging him to stick with natural history narratives, and it would be another five years until the final product was published with Oxford University Press.* In the letter rejecting the manuscript, Knopf's editor, Clinton Simpson, wrote: "I wonder if you would consider making a book purely of nature observations, with less emphasis on the ecological ideas which you have incorporated into your present manuscript?

---

* An excellent treatment of Leopold's struggle to find the right direction and format for his book is contained in "The Making of the Sand County Almanac" by Dennis Ribbens.

It seems to us that these ecological theories are very difficult indeed to present successfully for the layman. Certainly, the repetition in chapter after chapter of a book, of the idea that the various elements and forces of nature should be kept in balance would end by becoming monotonous."

What may well have daunted the publisher was Leopold's critical tone, which was something not commonly found in the natural history literature of the time. An example, from the section of sketches set in Wisconsin titled "Marshland Elegy," is this critique: "The high priests of progress knew nothing of cranes, and cared less. What is a species more or less among engineers? What good is an undrained marsh anyhow?" Such critiques probably sounded more edgy to his original audience, especially given the postwar ethos of triumph and prosperity. But Leopold's tone was moderated by his folksy voice. This voice is often expressed in side comments, such as in describing the "gangling, sorrel-colored young" of the Sandhill crane, where he ends with an aside: "These, albeit birds, are not properly called chicks, but *colts*. I have no idea why."*

Part of Leopold's brilliance is that he does not take a simplistic approach to conservation issues. He goes so far as to observe that "all conservation of wildness is self-defeating, for to cherish we must see and fondle, and when enough have seen and fondled, there is no wilderness left to cherish." The aversion to over-simplification here that may stem from Leopold's awareness of complex relationships within a given ecosystem, especially when scarcity is involved. He points out, for example, that clay-colored sparrows are found in the sand counties because they are enamored of jackpines, which in turn are enamored of sand. Likewise, he offers lighthearted speculation that the woodcocks prefer the sand environment because:

> The male woodcock, while doing his peenting prologue to the sky dance,
> is like a short lady in high heels: he does not show up to advantage in

---

* I suspect that in claiming that he had no idea why fledgling cranes were called "colts," Leopold was being facetious. A naturalist of his stature would know that young cranes are precocious and are able to run within twenty-four hours of hatching. Colt-like, they often jump in the process and at a very young age begin practicing their courtship dances even though they will not participate in mate selection for years. When Leopold calls the juveniles "sorrel-colored," he is using a color descriptor commonly applied to horses. It should be noted that adult male cranes are commonly called "roans" and adult females are called "mares." Their bluish-cray color is similar to that of a roan horse. Leopold was enough of an equestrian, going back to his days as a ranger in Arizona and New Mexico, to have made these connections.

dense tangled ground cover. But on the poorest sand-streak of the poorest pasture or meadow of the Sand Counties, there is, in April at least, no ground cover at all, save only moss, *Draba*, cardamine, sheep-sorrel, and *Antennaria*, all negligible impediments to a bird with short legs. Here the male woodcock can puff and strut and mince, not only without let or hindrance, but in full view of his audience, real or hoped-for.

As a group, the sketches get less notice these days than the other two sections of the book. This may in part be that that the information in them is more commonplace than it was when the book was published. "Odyssey," for example, traces the journey of a nitrogen atom cycling through the ecosystem, both in a healthy landscape and in an instance where nitrogen is washed away as a result of poor agricultural practices. The sketch would have been a solid way to learn about the nitrogen cycle for someone unschooled in biochemistry in 1949, but today an introduction to the cycle is usually included in the curriculum no later than the junior-high level, and its presentation in the sketch may seem a bit facile to modern students. This is a good thing.

The stand-out in terms of the sketches, "Thinking Like a Mountain," is in my opinion most notable and memorable of all Leopold's essays. It is also his most anthologized and commented-upon sketch, as well as the one most frequently assigned for student reading.

Prior to when this sketch was published, it was considered a truism in wildlife management that the more predators were killed, especially wolves, the more game animals would be available for hunters, especially deer and other ungulates. This viewpoint led to the extirpation of wolves throughout much of the continental United States and was even exported to other countries, such as Japan, leading to the extinction of wolves there.†

The sketch opens with reflections on the howl of a wolf and how it communicates meaning throughout a landscape. Then, a short narrative picks up about a time when Leopold and others were eating lunch one day, high up on a rimrock, when they saw a swimming wolf, which they had first mistaken for a deer, emerge from a river and be greeted by grown pups. Leopold explains that "in those days we had never heard of passing up a chance to kill a wolf," and so the group unloaded their rifles on the pack. What follows is one of the most oft-quoted paragraphs in

† The history of the intentional extinction of Japanese wolves can be found in Brett L. Walker, *The Lost Wolves of Japan* (Seattle: University of Washington Press, 2005).

American environmental literature: "We reached the old wolf in time to watch a fierce green fire dying in her eyes. I realized then, and have known ever since, that there was something new to me in those eyes—something known only to her and to the mountain. I was young then, and full of trigger-itch; I thought that because fewer wolves meant more deer, that no wolves would mean hunters' paradise. But after seeing the green fire die, I sensed that neither the wolf nor the mountain agreed with such a view."

The view Leopold espoused in this sketch was as unpopular among hunters and cattle ranchers as it tended to be with the wildlife management community, at least at first. He wrote that "just as a deer herd lives in mortal fear of its wolves, so does a mountain live in mortal fear of its deer." This fear comes from the fact that an unchecked deer population will overbrowse every edible bush and seedling, according to Leopold, who writes that he has also seen every edible tree "defoliated to the height of a saddlehorn," resulting in mass starvation.

It would take decades for the wildlife management community to understand that Leopold was right. In ecosystems such as Yellowstone National Park, where wolves were reintroduced, overbrowsing would be minimized, and the biotic community would be healthier overall, not just in terms of plants, but game animals as well. Today, "thinking like a mountain" has become code for taking a holistic view of ecosystems, especially in terms of understanding the ecological interconnections of each element of the system, especially keystone species.

The remaining sketches contain a critique of scientific progress at the expense of aesthetics, especially in terms of the demise of wilderness, and a warning about the spread of invasive species. There are also reflections on extinction, both local and global. The tone in these final sketches borders on the elegiac, most notably in the following passage: "Man always kills the thing he loves, and so we the pioneers have killed our wilderness. Some say we had to. Be that as it may, I am glad I shall never be young without wild country to be young in."

The third and final part of the book is called, appropriately, "The Upshot." Even on a first reading, one gets the sense that the most important part of the book is yet to come, that the fifteen essays in the first two parts, the almanac and the sketches, were a narrative prelude to a deeply philosophical climax. This is not to downplay the importance of the earlier essays to Leopold's rhetoric. We know from Leopold's correspondence that he wanted to document his own conversion in developing a conservation ethic. Further, the essays provide the foundation to his vision of ecological community upon which the land ethic will ultimately be based. The argument here moves from the descriptive (in Part I) to the expository (Part II) and then finally into the prescriptive (Part III.) It is a rhetorical movement where the author earns the right, in the reader's mind, to make a definitive statement at the end of the book. To jump directly into "The Land Ethic," as, regrettably, my own students would have to do in my survey class on environmental thought, was to miss the fullness of Leopold's persuasion.

Although Leopold will move expediently toward the ethical, it is significant that he begins "The Upshot" with aesthetic considerations; we will arrive at the land ethic via a path through a land aesthetic. This concern begins with a discussion of the burgeoning problem of outdoor recreation, which even in 1948 had become a motorized pursuit. He notes, "Everywhere is the unspecialized motorist whose recreation is mileage, who has run the gamut of the National Parks in one summer, and now is headed for Mexico City and points south." In one of his more lyrical sentences, Leopold complains, "*Homo sapiens* putters no more under his own vine and fig tree; he has poured into his gas tank the stored motivity of countless creatures aspiring through the ages to wiggle their way to pastures new. Ant-like he swarms the continents."

From a postwar perspective, Leopold predicts with great accuracy the mess that has become of outdoor recreation in the present day, with national parks overwhelmed by motorized campers, rivers dependent on hatchery trout raised specifically for recreational purposes, and game managers culling species such as herons and otters to ensure that they don't consume fish intended as trophies for well-furnished hobbyists. And this is precisely where Leopold moves into aesthetics, pointing out that recreation itself "is not the outdoors, but our reaction to it." He maintains that the only true development in our recreational resources is the development in the perceptive faculty of Americans. Critiquing development further, he maintains that "all of the other acts we grace by that name are, at best, attempts to retard or mask the process of dilution." This perceptive faculty can be attuned to infinitely small partitions, such as weeds in a city lot, without losing quality. To Leopold, those weeds convey the same lessons as the redwoods. This is something that what he calls the "trophy-recreationist" will never learn, something that will be that person's undoing.

In the final paragraph of this first essay of Part III, we find Leopold's complete aesthetic, one that is perhaps more relevant today than it was seventy-five years ago: "It would appear, in short, that the rudimentary grades of outdoor recreation consume their resource-base; the higher grades, at least to a degree, create their own satisfactions with little or no attrition of land or life. It is the expansion of transport without a corresponding growth of perception that threatens us with qualitative bankruptcy of the recreational process. Recreational development is a job not of building roads into lovely country, but of building receptivity into the still unlovely human mind."

In the next chapter, "Wildlife in American Culture," Leopold turns toward ethics without abandoning aesthetics. He embraces the contribution that hunting has contributed to American culture but, at the same time, bemoans the fact that "the gadgeteer, otherwise known as the sporting-goods dealer," has draped the American outdoorsman with "an infinity of contraptions, all offered as aids to self-reliance, hardihood, woodcraft, or marksmanship, but too often functioning as substitutes for them." As a case in point, he portrays the modern duck hunter thus: "As an end-case consider the duck-hunter, sitting in a steel boat behind composition decoys. A put-put motor has brought him to the blind without exercise. Canned heat stands by to warm him in case of a chilling wind. He talks to the passing flocks on a factory caller, in what he hopes are seductive tones; home lessons from a phonograph record have taught him how."

Leopold proposes two solutions, the first being a code of sportsmanship with self-imposed limitations on sport. These limitations would enhance American values such as marksmanship. The second would be voluntary adherence to ethical codes that generate self-respect, such as a common denominator of all sporting codes not to waste good meat. As regards this second solution, he points out the number of Wisconsin deer hunters who, in pursuit of a legal buck, "kill and abandon in the woods at least one doe, fawn, or spike buck for every two legal bucks taken out."

Toward the end of the essay, Leopold also proposes a new sort of sport, wildlife research, where he extols the value of "amateur research." This is something that has finally come to fruition, albeit under a more marketable name, "citizen science." As a strong proponent of citizen science, I can attest that it was my favorite form of outdoor recreation back when I was a member of a hawkwatch team, even though I never conceptualized this activity as sport.

In the third essay of the "Upshot" section, Leopold discusses wilderness, which he described as "the raw material out of which man has hammered the artifact of civilization." He makes a number of arguments for wilderness preservation, the most compelling of which is the preservation of habitat for wildlife. But he also returns to the aesthetic, especially with this remarkable sentence: "Ability to see the cultural value of wilderness boils down, in the last analysis, to a question of intellectual humility." It is this humility that reminds us how we are rooted to the land and helps us understand that "all history consists of successive excursions from a single starting-point, to which man returns again and again to organize yet another search for a durable scale of values. It is only the scholar who understands why the raw wilderness gives definition and meaning to the human enterprise."

That point having been made, there is one chapter left in *A Sand Count Almanac*, and it is the book's most consequential chapter: "The Land Ethic."

The foundation for Leopold's ethic lies in what he calls "the community concept." In his hypothesis, he claims that all ethics evolve from a sense of responsibility that individuals owe the community in which they live. His land ethic "simply enlarges the boundaries of the community to include soils, waters, plants, and animals, or collectively, the land." He will move this theory one step more by asserting that the task before us is to extend social conscience from people to land, at which point society will recognize the obligations it has toward the biotic community.

At the risk of oversimplifying, I would rephrase the foundation of the land ethic thus: we must move from considering the land a commodity to viewing it as a biotic community that includes us, a community to which we have ethical obligations. These obligations go beyond whatever we perceive as the economic values of that biotic community. Leopold goes so far as to assert that "a system of conservation based solely on economic self-interest is hopelessly lopsided" because it tends to ignore elements of the land community that may lack commercial value but are essential to the healthy functioning of the ecosystem. For this system to work, the resulting ethical obligations must be felt by the private land owner as well as by government agencies charged with maintaining the land. Here, Leopold cautions, "We can be ethical only in relationship to something we can see, feel, understand, love, or otherwise have faith in."

At this point Leopold introduces the concept of a land pyramid where we can perceive land as a biotic mechanism. He finds this more productive than the image of the balance of nature. By understanding land as an interconnected system of food chains where energy flows upward from primary producers to secondary or tertiary consumers, we arrive at three realizations: (1) that the land is not merely soil; (2) that native plants and animals keep the energy circuit open while non-native organisms might not; (3) that anthropogenic changes are of a different order than evolutionary changes, and often have unforeseen effects.

In Leopold's system, "health" is the capacity of the land for self-renewal. He is not using health as a metaphor here, but rather is talking about communal health, the health of the biotic community. That capacity for self-renewal is what modern ecologists call "resilience," but that's not a term Leopold uses in *A Sand County Almanac*. Regardless, Leopold defines conservation as our effort to understand and preserve the capacity for self-renewal.

The final section of "The Land Ethic" is called "The Outlook," and it is obvious that Leopold invested considerable effort drafting his argument. Consider how the rhetoric tightens in the topic sentences of the first three paragraphs of this section:

1. "It is inconceivable to me that an ethical relation to land can exist without love, respect, and admiration for land, and a high regard for its value."

2. "Perhaps the most serious obstacle impeding the evolution of a land ethic is the fact that our educational and economic system is headed away from, rather than toward, an intense consciousness of land."

3. "One of the requisites for an ecological comprehension of land is an understanding of ecology, and this is by no means co-extensive with 'education'; in fact, much higher education seems deliberately to avoid ecological concepts."

It is at the end of the fourth paragraph, however, that the land ethic is finally defined: "A thing is right when it tends to preserve the integrity, stability, and beauty of the biotic community. It is wrong when it tends otherwise."*

Note here that the conjunction used in Leopold's capsule of the land ethic is "and" rather than "or." A thing doesn't become right by preserving the integrity, stability, *or* beauty of the biotic community. It must tend to preserve all three—and note as well that aesthetic considerations were not just the starting point of the land ethic, but an applied element as well. The biotic community's beauty must be preserved along with its integrity and stability. Without that beauty, it will be hard for the human element of the biotic community to develop its love, respect, and admiration of the land.

Having struggled for years to find a home for *A Sand County Almanac*, in April of 1948, Leopold finally received the news that Oxford University Press would publish the book. Exactly one week later, while battling a grass fire on a

---

* I used to award my students a two-point bonus on the exam if they committed that definition to memory. For some, it was the only thing they'd had to memorize during their collegiate careers.

neighbor's property near his beloved shack, Aldo Leopold died of a heart attack. His second eldest son, Luna B. Leopold, saw the manuscript through the editing and production process so that it could be published posthumously.

The Sea Around Us by Rachel Carson (1951)

> Wonder and humility are wholesome emotions, and they do not exist side by side
> with a lust for destruction. —FROM *LOST WOODS*

In 1907, President Theodore Roosevelt sent off a fleet of sixteen white-painted battleships to circumnavigate the globe in a display of American naval might. Over the course of that year, seven national forests—Nantahala, Colville, Umpqua, Custer, Inyo, Chugach, and Ouachita—would be established by the Roosevelt administration. In 1907, Robert Service debuted his first collection of poetry, *The Spell of the Yukon and Other Verses*, which surged through sixteen printings in its first year. That summer Annette Kellerman, an Australian long-distance swim champion, was arrested and charged with indecent exposure at Boston's Revere Beach after swimming in a one-piece bathing suit that didn't include a skirt. The first electric washing machine was introduced by the Hurley Machine Company of Chicago in 1907, and Rachel Carson was born.

Carson began writing animal stories at the age of eight and had her first story published at the age of ten in the *St. Nicholas Magazine*. She went to the Pennsylvania College for Women to study English,* but switched her major to biology, having come under the mentorship of a teacher, Mary Scott Skinker, in that

---

* The school had been chartered in 1869 as the Pennsylvania Female College, but the name was changed to the Pennsylvania College of Women in 1890, and then to Chatham College in 1955. It has been known as Chatham University since 2007.

subject. Carson eventually specialized in marine biology and ultimately earned a master's degree in zoology from Johns Hopkins. She was interested in pursuing a doctorate, but her father's illness, combined with the Great Depression, precluded that option when she became her mother's sole supporter. She started writing articles about marine life in the Chesapeake, publishing in both magazines and newspapers, which lead to work with the US Bureau of Fisheries and, subsequently, with the US Fish and Wildlife Service, where she became editor of publications. During that time, however, she took an interest in writing books. Her first, *Under the Sea Wind: A Naturalist's Picture of Ocean Life*, received excellent reviews but sold poorly. Undaunted, she wrote a second book, *The Sea Around Us*, which became a *New York Times* bestseller for eighty-six weeks, having spent thirty-one weeks on the top of the list. At that point, she was able to quit her job and write full time. A third book, *Edge of the Sea*, also became a bestseller, its sales surpassing the previous book.

Despite the success of Carson's ocean trilogy, most students of environmental literature are more conversant with her book, *Silent Spring*, an exposé warning of the environmental dangers of chlorinated hydrocarbons, a book that ultimately led to a ban on DDT in most countries. While *Silent Spring* may indeed be Carson's masterwork, I have not included it in this study because it is not a work of literary natural history, even though it contains literary elements, especially in terms of its first chapter, which is named "A Fable for Tomorrow." However, I would classify *Silent Spring* more generally as environmental writing, not only because it was not written for literary pleasure but also because it does not incorporate the experiences of the naturalist into the text.* Without wanting to detract anything from the importance of *Silent Spring,* especially in terms of how vital it was in saving a few of my favorite birds from extinction—the osprey, peregrine falcon, bald eagle, and California condor—I argue here that *Silent Spring* was largely made possible by the success of Carson's more literary work, books that gave her a national audience and an elevated platform from which to point out the problems that pesticides can wreak in the environment.

The *Sea Around Us* won the National Book Award for Nonfiction in 1952, and the John Burroughs Medal for nature writing.† It has been translated into

---

* The more recent the literary natural history, the more difficult it becomes to distinguish between activist and literary work. Of the four characteristics of literary natural history discussed in this book's preface, the primary difference between *Silent Spring* and the ten works included in this study would be the incorporation of the naturalist in the text.

† Two other writers included in this study have been awarded the Burroughs Medal: Aldo Leopold and Robin Wall Kimmerer.

twenty-eight languages. A film version was made in 1952 and won an Academy Award for Best Documentary the following year. (Carson's biographer, Linda Lear, notes that despite the Oscar, Carson was so disappointed with the script that she decided never again to sell the film rights to any of her books. This alone should inform us about Rachel Carson's lifelong commitment to getting content right.)

Carson's writing was always heavily researched, and she never compromised on the science to make *The Sea Around Us* more accessible. Regardless, the payoff for the reader is that so much of the content revealed a little-known realm, presented in such a fashion that the prose held the interest of a broad audience, novice through expert. The brilliance here is that a book containing so much science could become a bestseller. Carson made her approach work because behind the science there is always a subtext of wonder—the author's unending amazement at the natural world.

The following sentences, taken from the opening paragraph of the chapter "The Changing Year," are exemplary of this subtext:

> For the sea as a whole, the alternation of day and night, the passage of the seasons, the procession of the years, are lost in its vastness, obliterated in its own changeless eternity. But the surface waters are different. The face of the sea is always changing. Crossed by colors, lights, and moving shadows, sparkling in the sun, mysterious in the twilight, its aspects and its moods vary hour by hour. The surface waters move with the tides, stir to the breath of the winds, and rise and fall to the endless, hurrying forms of the waves. Most of all, they change with the advance of the seasons.

Note, in the above passage, how the dynamism of the ocean's surface is expressed metaphorically, employing such phrases as: "the face of the sea," "its aspects and its moods," "the endless, hurrying forms of the waves," language that often crosses into anthropomorphism. The reader knows that science is forthcoming, but discovers it always to be accompanied by appreciation of the sublime qualities of the seascape. When Carson shows us the science, it is inevitably accompanied by her personal aesthetic.

The Sea Around Us was not the first oceanographic book to be well-received by the American public. William Beebe, best known as the co-designer of the bathysphere in which he set ocean depth records in the 1930s and who conducted research for the New York Zoological Society throughout his career, published a number of popular texts about the marine environment, including *Beneath Tropic Seas* (1928), *Nonsuch: Land of Water* (1932), *Half Mile Down* (1934), *Zaca Venture*

(1938), and *Book of Bays* (1934). Although his biggest seller was *Half Mile Down*, my favorite among those books has always been *Zaca Venture,* no doubt because the natural history is explored during an ocean voyage aboard a wooden-hulled schooner bound for the Sea of Cortez.

Carson was deeply grateful to Beebe, who had included an essay written by her in his *The Book of Naturalists: An Anthology of the Best Natural History*, published in 1945 when she was relatively unknown. She dedicated the first edition of *The Sea Around Us* to him, writing: "My absorption in the mystery and meaning of the sea have been stimulated and the writing of this book aided by the friendship and encouragement of William Beebe."

The Rachel Carson of 1951 wrote more as a naturalist, and less as an environmentalist, than had she written the book ten years later. The preface to the second edition, published in 1961, gives evidence of this, especially in terms of eight final paragraphs, which deal with the danger of nuclear waste disposal in the ocean environment.* Carson summarizes that section with a dire warning:

> The problem, then, is far more complex and far more hazardous than has been admitted. Even in the comparatively short time since disposal began, research has shown that some of the assumptions on which it was based were dangerously inaccurate. The truth is that disposal has proceeded far more rapidly than our knowledge justifies. To dispose first and investigate later is an invitation to disaster, for once radioactive elements have been deposited at sea they are irretrievable. The mistakes that are made now are made for all time.

In comparing *The Sea Around Us* to *Silent Spring*, the earlier book clearly surpasses the later in terms of lyricism as well as in evoking the sublime. This emphasis can be understood as well in terms of the role science plays in each book. While in *Silent Spring* the science tends to create a sense of apprehension and foreboding, in *The Sea Around Us* it tends to stimulate wonder and marvel. Carson takes us beyond the chemistry, the physics, and the geology of the marine world to a place where readers can experience the underwater environment with their imaginations, such as in this passage:

---

* The United States had been dumping radioactive waste into the ocean as early as 1946, and did not stop the practice until 1970 at the recommendation of the U.S. Council on Environmental Quality. The USA signed and ratified the London Dumping Convention in 1972.

Down beyond the reach of the sun's rays, there is no alternation of light and darkness. There is rather an endless night, as old as the sea itself. For most of its creatures, groping their way endlessly through its black waters, it must be a place of hunger, where food is scarce and hard to find, a shelterless place where there is no sanctuary from ever-present enemies, where one can only move on and on, from birth to death, through the darkness, confined as in a prison to his own particular layer of the sea.

The operative phrase, when one close-reads the above passage, is "it must be." Here Carson is describing something that we can never fully experience, a lifetime of darkness, and she can't definitively describe it because such a lifetime is beyond anything she could have experienced personally. She therefore invites us to accompany her on an imaginal voyage, employing phrases like "it must be a place of hunger." That sentence envisions a series of placements in the abysmal marine environment: a place of hunger and scarcity; a shelterless place without safe haven; a place where the darkness is inescapable; a place of confinement. By the end of the paragraph, the readers feel they somehow know the place and have in some way learned the unknowable. And yet most of us are probably glad at this point that we can come up for air in the sunlight.

As I have reread the various books included in this study, none has given me as much unexpected pleasure as my recent reading of *The Sea Around Us*. This time I've becoming aware of how Carson explores her subject matter as an interdisciplinary scholar. Her presentation of how our knowledge of the deep-sea abyss has evolved, for example, turns to the historical undermining of misconceptions, starting with the question, "They used to say that nothing could live in the deep sea. It was a belief that must have been easy to accept, for without proof to the contrary, how could anyone conceive of life in such a place?" From there, she reaches back a century, to the point where British biologist Edward Forbes postulated that because the sea's inhabitants become fewer and fewer at increased depths, there must be a point where all life is extinguished. From there, she moves to the early nineteenth century, to the 1818 Arctic explorations of Sir John Ross, who managed to dredge mud containing worms from a depth of one thousand fathoms, thus proving that there was animal life in the ocean "notwithstanding the darkness, stillness, silence, and immense pressure produced by more than a mile of superincumbent water." She then skips to 1860, when the sounding line of the survey ship *Bulldog* came up from 1,260 fathoms with thirteen starfish clinging to it, prompting the ship's naturalist to note that "the deep has sent up a long coveted message." Her historical exploration continues through the *Challenger* expedition of 1872, to early echo soundings of the twentieth century, to fishermen using fathometers in the 1930s, and finally into discoveries of the deep scattering layer in the 1940s by various expeditions, including the naval vessel *USS Jasper* and the research vessel *E. W. Scripps*. While the reader learns science throughout this dissertation, that learning comes via the discourse of history. Carson's approach here is not only interdisciplinary but also transdisciplinary, developing a single intellectual framework that unites the humanities and the sciences.

Carson was so aware of the vast multidisciplinary nature of the book that she sometimes jokingly referred to its title as *Out of my Depth*, or *Carson at Sea*.

Carson delights in pointing out that over time humans were discovering secrets that animals already knew, from sperm whales that descend more than five hundred fathoms to feed on giant squid, to northern fur seals, whose stomachs have contained the bones of deepwater fish unknown to science. Similarly, Carson shows how our lack of knowledge about ocean habitats has sometimes foiled underwater technology, such as when the United States Navy set up a hydrophone network at the mouth of the Chesapeake Bay during World War II to detect enemy incursion into those waters. That network was made useless when it went live in 1942; every evening it detected constant noises that sounded like a pneumatic drill tearing up pavement. This noise turned out to be biotic in origin, the voice of croaker fish that move into the Chesapeake each spring from their offshore wintering grounds. The ambient clamor was so loud that it completely masked mechanical noise, at least until the Navy figured out how to screen out the croakers via an electronic filter.

Carson treats deep-sea organisms as exotic creatures, especially fish. She writes of a fishing trawl bringing up a latimeria, a fish thought to have been extinct for sixty million years, and of frillsharks, which are more similar to ancient sharks that swam the oceans thirty million years ago than to modern sharks. In the same breath, she tells of the development of the bathyscaphe, a deep-sea vessel developed by Auguste Piccard, a Swiss physicist, that was capable of exploring the Mariana Trench to a depth of 35,800 feet, nearly seven miles. We can only imagine the effect Carson's exotic descriptions had with an audience in the 1950s, in an age before film technology could record images from the abyss and when the bulk of underwater exploration was still conducted by the military. Even seventy years later, I find her descriptions of continental shelfs and underwater topography enlightening, and as a writer I admire the depth of research that Carson must have undertaken behind almost every page of the book. If some of this knowledge is now commonplace—and most of it is not—we can perhaps thank Carson for bringing it to light, at least to the general public.

Sixty-some pages into the book, Carson evoked a perspective of geologic time, exploring how oceanographers had developed the methodologies of coring the ocean floor and examining the contents of these cores. She portrays the ocean floor as always receiving sediment deposits as if they were a snowstorm, and asks a question that may be even more pertinent now than it was at the time of publication: "It is interesting to think that even now, in our own lifetime, the flakes of a new snow storm are falling, falling, one by one, out there on the ocean floor. The billions of Globigerina are drifting down, writing their unequivocal record that this, our present world, is on the whole a world of mild and temperate climate. Who will read their record, ten thousand years from now?"

For those of us who initially became acquainted with Rachel Carson through her landmark work, *Silent Spring*, a book sometimes credited with starting the environmental movement, one of the surprises of reading *The Sea Around* Us may be the earlier work's relative lack of environmental advocacy. This is not a book primarily concerned about issues such as pollution, overfishing, ocean acidification, or the destruction of marine habitats. Quite simply, the woman who warned the world of the dangers of chlorinated hydrocarbons in pesticides was not yet at a point in her writing career where general environmental issues had aroused her activism. The singular exception to this in the first edition of *The Sea Around Us* is where Carson dedicates seven pages of the chapter "The Birth of an Island" to a historical look at how humans have devastated numerous island ecologies by introducing non-native plants and animals. She writes:

> But man, unhappily, has written one of his blackest records as a destroyer on the oceanic islands. He has seldom set foot on an island that he has not brought about disastrous changes. He has destroyed environments by cutting, clearing, and burning; he has brought with him as a chance associate the nefarious rat; and almost invariably he has turned loose upon the islands a whole Noah's Ark of goats, hogs, cattle, dogs, cats, and other non-native animals as well as plants. Upon species after species of island life, the black night of extinction has fallen.

Those seven pages amount to little more than an environmental scolding directed broadly at humanity, however, and do not represent a major area of concern for the book. The point of *The Sea Around Us* is to fascinate its readers in such a way as to stimulate greater concern for the ecosystem. As it is, the sea trilogy serves as a series of three comprehensive surveys, each distinct, each providing an education in marine ecology, and yet each aware that there is great mystery that permeates a historical moment, both in terms of awareness and discovery. That said, I would caution against conceiving the scarcity of environmental concern to be a blind spot in Carson's early writing, especially in *The Sea Around Us*. Rather, I view the development of her interdisciplinary approach as being the building block of her evolving environmentalism. She is not merely the marine biologist she was typically characterized as being: she was also a capable geologist, oceanographer, naturalist, historian of science, and—as we finally discovered in *Silent Spring*—an investigative chemist. It is in the aggregation of such disparate concerns that an environmental ethos is generated. It was coming, and it was coming soon.

The works within the trilogy pursue completely different narrative strategies, divergent approaches to blending imagination and expertise. The first book, *Under the Sea Wind*, is structured as a series of stories told from the point of view of various marine organisms. To Carson, the central character of the book was the ocean itself, and the book takes on a dreamy, cinematic quality that borders on being fantastical. This contrasts sharply with the second book, which as we have seen deals with the ocean as a vast macrocosm that science was in the early stages of understanding. The third installation, *The Edge of the Sea*, restricts itself to the liminal zone, the area between the high and low tide lines, thus dealing with microcosm rather than macrocosm. The various liminal landscapes—the beach, the rocky shores, the tide pools—explore "compromise, conflict and eternal change" in a spirit of attentiveness and discovery. Carson's mastery, in short, was in the fact that a succession of four books could be so distinct from each other, not just in terms of disciplinary focus, but in the scope of the writing itself. One could posit that Carson wrote *Silent Spring* because she was uniquely capable of writing a book unlike anything that had been written before. And it helped that she had an enthusiastic base of readers who were willing to follow her even into the urgent abyss of chemistry.

If the ghost of Rachel Carson had the opportunity to come back in the present and revise any single chapter in *The Sea Around Us*, I suspect she would want to rewrite "The Shape of Ancient Seas," which concludes Part I of the book and begins with the sentence, "We live in an age of rising seas." Carson notes that along the Atlantic seaboard the sea-level rise amounted to "about a third of a foot" between 1930 and 1948. Then she comments, "This evidence of a rising sea is an interesting and even an exciting thing because it is rare that, in the short span of human life, we can actually observe and measure the progress of one of the great earth rhythms. What is happening is nothing new." When Carson makes the case that nothing new is happening, she does so specifically in terms of the long span of geologic time, but also mentions that only in recent decades have there been instruments such as tide gauges that could measure ocean rise. Then she states, "Where and when the ocean will halt its present advance and begin again its slow retreat into its basin, no one can say." We must remember that those words were published in 1951, and that Gilbert Plass's seminal paper, "The Carbon Dioxide Theory of Climate Change," which definitively linked increases in carbon dioxide in the atmosphere–ocean system to global warming, wasn't published until 1956. However, when Carson updated the book for its 1960 second addition, she apparently still believed that the causes of ocean rise she had written about should be attributed to geological processes rather than anthropogenic climate change.

In Part II of the book, "The Restless Sea," Carson shifts the emphasis away from geology to dynamic systems, such as wind, waves, tides and currents. Here again she engages in discourses other than the life sciences in which she trained, and yet she does so with expertise and aplomb. At a time when the sciences were specializing expeditiously, especially in terms of research methodologies, Carson demonstrated a remarkable transdisciplinary capacity, both in terms of being able to synthesize a wide spectrum of research, as well as in being able to communicate effectively to a general audience about discoveries outside of her disciplinary specialty. Such an approach would not become the norm in such interdisciplinary fields as environmental studies until the next generation of scholars.

The third and final section of the book, "Man and the Sea about Him," begins with a chapter about how the ocean functions as a great regulator of temperatures. Carson explains how the ocean is an excellent absorber and radiator of heat, and makes the case that without the ocean, the world would experience "unthinkably harsh extremes of temperature." Building on her disquisition about ocean currents in the book's middle section, she discusses how heat and cold can be distributed over thousands of miles, not only by current but by atmospheric effects as well, positing that "the redistribution of heat for the whole earth is accomplished about half by the ocean currents, and half by the winds." At this point, she gets into a protracted discussion about how much Arctic waters had warmed recently, both in terms of the loss of sea ice and northern glaciers, but attributes this to climactic cycles:

Unquestionably, there are other agents at work in bringing about the climatic changes in the Arctic and sub-Arctic regions. For one thing, it is almost certainly true that we are still in the warming-up stage following the last Pleistocene glaciation—that the world's climate, over the next thousands of years, will grow considerably warmer before beginning a downward swing into another Ice Age. But what we are experiencing now is perhaps a climatic change of shorter duration, measurable only in decades or centuries.

The following chapter, "Wealth from the Salt Seas," which is the penultimate chapter of the book, is the one I find the most troubling from an ecocritical perspective. It catalogues a number of mineral resources that are routinely extracted from the sea, including iodine, bromine, magnesium, salt, and petroleum, the latter of which Carson calls the most valuable "legacy" of the ancient seas. She points out that petroleum "is a result of fundamental earth processes that have been operating ever since an abundant and varied life was developed in the sea—at least since the beginning of Paleozoic time, probably longer." The book goes on for ten pages about how much oil the seas contain, and about the exploration for undersea oil, but cautions that it is no simple matter to obtain oil from undersea fields, at that point sounding as if it were written by a publicist employed by the oil extraction industry. Clearly, the 1950s mindset, bent upon a postwar mentality where the American dream finally neared its two-cars-in-every-garage ideal, saw petroleum extraction through a different lens than one finds in contemporary environmental thought.

As if she hadn't already dazzled her readers with interdisciplinary expertise, Carson used her final chapter, "The Encircling Sea," to explore the history of oceanic navigation, starting with the ancient Greeks dating back to Homer. Over the course of the chapter she references classical authorities such as Herodotus, Himilco of Carthage, the Roman Avienus, Pytheas of Massalia, the Arab geographer al-Idrisi, Adam of Bremen, and the geographer Posidonius, once again exceeding the scope of knowledge one would expect of a marine biologist. It's little wonder that the general reading public was ready to accept her expertise when it came to the issues that would be dealt with in *Silent Spring*.

As of this point, seven decades after its publication, The *Sea Around Us* has been relegated to a minor, partially outdated work that's primarily of interest to scholars. It has become little more than a footnote exemplifying the sort of literature Carson preferred to write prior to taking up *Silent Spring*, reluctantly, at first, as an advocacy project. I would argue, however, that such a viewpoint fails to appreciate *The Sea Around Us* on its own merits. Even had *Silent Spring* never been published, Carson would still have made a major contribution to the scope of literary natural history, especially in terms of the ability to engage a general audience deeply in technical material.

Regardless of the above, when *Silent Spring* was published it had such a profound effect on environmental literature that it's difficult to appreciate Carson's earlier work without prejudice. At best, the literary critic might ask how the two works may have related to each other within the author's mind. A clue to this might be found in Carson's acceptance speech upon receiving the John Burroughs Medal for *The Sea Around Us*:

> I myself am convinced that there has never been a greater need than there is today for the reporter and interpreter of the natural world. Mankind has gone very far into an artificial world of his own creation. He has sought to insulate himself, in his cities of steel and concrete, from the realities of earth and water and the growing seed. Intoxicated with a sense of his own power, he seems to be going farther and farther into more experiments for the destruction of himself and his world.

To the extent that Carson saw her role to be a reporter and interpreter of the natural world, it can be argued that she'd filled these roles in both *The Sea Around Us* and *Silent Spring*. In the former work, she had reported on a world little known to the general populace, a world of depth and darkness where humans were almost entirely out of their element. The later work essentially takes place in the reader's back yard, a world of birdsong and sunshine where hidden perils were causing levels of devastation that few people understood, and many scientists denied. Both ecosystems called for a naturalist to report on the environmental processes at work and to interpret the natural history as a dynamic system, a system that humanity was part of, not above.

Both books, ultimately, changed how we read nature. *The Sea Around Us* challenged our propensity to read nature as being primarily a terrestrial phenomenon, at best a thing surrounded by water. The general public could suddenly perceive how such phenomena as marine currents or the sediment of the ocean floor effected the entire planetary ecosystem. *Silent Spring* changed how we read nature by revealing the fragility of ecosystems at the hands of modern technology, especially in terms of biocides that we'd been assured were harmless.

Desert Solitaire: A Season in the Wilderness by Edward Abbey (1968)

> I dream of a hard and brutal mysticism in which the naked self merges with the nonhuman world and yet somehow survives still intact, individual, separate. Paradox and bedrock. —FROM THE CHAPTER, "THE FIRST MORNING"

In 1927, Charles Lindbergh made the first transatlantic flight in his single-engine aircraft, the Spirit of St. Louis, Philo T. Farnsworth transmitted the first electronic television signal,* Babe Ruth hit sixty home runs, the Ford Motor Company manufactured the fifteen-millionth-and-final Model T, carving began on the sculptures on Mount Rushmore, and the Harlem Globetrotters were founded. William Falkner's satiric novel, *Mosquitos*, was published, as was Ernest Hemmingway's second collection of short stories, *Men without Women*. Willa Cather's historical novel, *Death Comes for the Archbishop*, was published to critical acclaim, and Edward Abbey was born in Home, Pennsylvania.

Technically, according to his birth certificate, Abbey was born in Indiana, Pennsylvania, but he so liked the name of the neighboring village, "Home," that he claimed it as his birthplace. A state historical marker in Home testifies that, while Abbey was born in Indiana, PA, he grew up "in and around the village of Home."

The fact that there is confusion about Abbey's place of birth—confusion between what actually happened and what is claimed to have happened—says a

---

* Philo Taylor Farnsworth was a first cousin of my grandfather, Philo Yates Farnsworth. According to family tradition, the firstborn son was always to be named Philo, followed by the mother's maiden name. My name, thus, should have been Philo Seibert Farnsworth, had not my parents broken with this custom.

lot about the author himself. In Abbey's case, the author holding the pen is not identical to the Edward Abbey being written about: the narrator is a construct of the narrative itself, with a personality distinct from that of the real author. Abbey scholars have labelled this implied author "Cactus Ed," and, in my own scholarship, I've analyzed Cactus Ed as a rhetorical construct of the author, Edward Abbey. Were they brilliant? Yes. Factual? Almost. We can truly say that Cactus Ed was born in Home, even though Edward Abbey was not.

What most differentiates Abbey from the other authors critiqued in this study is that he did not consider himself a naturalist. Abbey devotes the entire introduction of his book of essays, *The Journey Home: Some Words in Defense of the American West,* supporting the claim made in its first sentence: "I am not a naturalist." At one point, he expands this claim to the entire genre of literary natural history, writing, "Several years ago I published a book called *Desert Solitaire,* followed closely by *Cactus Country, Appalachian Wilderness,* and *Slickrock.* Although classified by librarians as 'nature books,' they belong to the category of personal history not natural history." He goes on to claim that these nonfiction books are mostly "simple narrative accounts of travel and adventure, with philosophical commentary added here and there to give the prose a high-toned surface gleam. They have little to do with biological science." In the following paragraph, he goes so far as to suggest, "So much for the mantle and britches of Thoreau and Muir. Let Annie Dillard wear them now." (Dillard's writing is the subject of the next chapter in this study.)

In *Desert Solitaire,* Abbey adopted a countercultural perspective from the vantage of a seasonal wilderness ranger dissatisfied with the way federal parklands were being managed. He intended the writing to be provocative, and he seemed energized by the fact that his book would not fit into an existing framework. Writing of the book's rough edges in its introduction, he predicted that many would find it to be flawed:

> Certain faults will be obvious to the general reader, of course, and for these I wish to apologize. I quite agree that much of the book will seem coarse, rude, bad-tempered, violently prejudiced, unconstructive—even frankly antisocial in its point of view. Serious critics, serious librarians, serious associate professors of English will if they read this work dislike it intensely; at least I hope so. To others I can only say that if the book has virtues they cannot be disentangled from the faults; that there is a way of being wrong which is also sometimes necessarily right.

Having thus set the reader up to expect something dismal, the first sentence of the first chapter seems designed to take anyone who'd read the introduction by surprise: "This is the most beautiful place on earth." Abbey goes on to describe his first encounter with his remote ranger station, a trailer twenty miles off the paved road. He tells first of coming to a modest signboard that warns of quicksand and instructs the traveler not to cross the wash when the water is running. Observing that the wash looked perfectly dry in his headlights, Abbey crosses it, and arrives in a landscape where he glimpses "weird humps of pale rock on either side, like petrified elephants, dinosaurs, stone-age hobgoblins."

What Abbey is doing here, somewhat masterfully, is evoking desert terrain. He is not describing it the way a naturalist might but is rather setting the scene the way a novelist would. Of course, before writing *Desert Solitaire*, which was his first work of nonfiction other than for an unpublished master's thesis about anarchy and the morality of violence, Abbey had published three novels, the second two of which were set in the desert southwest. In Abbey's sparse description of finally arriving at his trailer, the language matches the setting: "A cold night, a cold wind, the snow falling like confetti. In the lights of the truck I unlocked the housetrailer, got out bedroll and baggage and moved in. By flashlight I found the bed, unrolled my sleeping bag, pulled off my boots and crawled in and went to sleep at once."

Abbey switches to present tense, however, when he finally steps outside in the pre-sunrise first light of the following morning:

> Time to get dressed, get out and have a look at the lay of the land, fix a breakfast. I try to pull on my boots but they're stiff as iron from the cold. I light a burner on the stove and hold the boots upside down above the flame until they are malleable enough to force my feet into. I put on a coat and step outside. Into the center of the world, God's navel, Abbey's country, the red wasteland.

"Abbey's country" tells us everything we need to know about this red wasteland. It suits him: a cantankerous man occupies a cantankerous landscape that he hopes will never change. It's just right the way it is, and that's the foundation of Abbey's argument in favor of leaving parkland undeveloped, especially parkland situated in Abbey's country. It suits him.

Abbey describes a few of the arches he can see from his doorstep, as well as a fifty-foot-high balanced rock mounted on a pedestal that he tells us looks like "a stone god or a petrified ogre." Then he asks himself whether this is how he really wants to describe things: "Like a god, like an ogre? The personification of the natural is exactly the tendency I wish to suppress in myself, to eliminate for good."

The reader learns quickly not to take Abbey at his word; he turns out not to have made a sustained effort to avoid the personification of nature. As I wrote long ago in a rhetorical analysis of *Desert Solitaire*:

> In the lexicon of *Desert Solitaire*, the wind breathes, the sun roars and daylight itself is full of tyranny. Gnats are described as "embittered little bastards," a turkey vulture is aptly described as "Cousin Buzzard," and quicksand has a "sinister glamour." The coyotes' repertoire, in part, is comprised of "occult music." The desert transmogrifies into "a pink world being sunburned to death." The Colorado River is not only "imperturbable" but is also described as having no false pride. At one point, four consecutive adjectival personifications will be needed to describe the "steady, powerful, unhurried, insouciant Colorado." Conversely, the personality of one of the Colorado's tributaries, the Escalante, somehow becomes "totally different, strange, unknown and unknowable, faintly malevolent."

Abbey's lack of reliability has confounded scholars for years. For example, in the introduction of *Desert Solitaire* he claims to have taken most of the book's contents "direct and unchanged" from his journals. As grad student, I went to considerable lengths to gain access to Abbey's journals from 1956 and 1957, the years he served as a ranger at what was then Arches National Monument,* and I discovered that very little of the content of the book came directly from the journals. I also discovered that some of what he writes about in the book is directly contradicted by what he'd written in the journals. In the journals, for example, he writes of his loneliness dozens of times, and yet in the book he writes of being twenty miles from the next human being "but instead of loneliness I feel loveliness. Loveliness and quiet exultation." Similarly, at the beginning of his second summer at Arches, Abbey writes in his journal, "Back in Abbey's country again. I walk in beauty. I go in beauty. Once again. And this time my wife and my son shall share it with me." He never once mentions the presence of wife and son in the book, however. After all, that would work against the trope of the solitary desert rambler to which Cactus Ed subscribes.

---

* The monument was designated a national park by President Richard Nixon in 1971.

Surprisingly, despite the content of *Desert Solitaire* not being trustworthy in many instances, this is overcome by the vigor of Abbey's writing combined with the provocative nature of the book's contentions. He struck a chord with a young generation of outdoor enthusiasts who were increasingly wary of governmental agencies, not only because of dishonesty about the safety of such things as DDT but also because, by the time *Desert Solitaire* was published in 1968, the Vietnam War had become hugely unpopular with the generation that was being called upon to fight in it. Our political system seemed in chaos; Martin Luther King Jr. and Robert Kennedy were both assassinated the year *Desert Solitaire* was published. Abbey came along with a countercultural message at the precise moment when it would best resonate.

Desert Solitaire's third chapter, "Serpents of Paradise," begins with Abbey sitting on the stoop of his trailer early one morning, drinking coffee. He looks down between his boots and sees there a rattlesnake, which he clarifies is a "horny rattler,"† which he further identifies as a "Faded Midget," not a diamondback. The correct common name would be "midget faded rattlesnake," and we have no way of knowing whether Abbey knew the correct terminology and opted for a name that sounded better to him, or whether he just got it wrong. The author contemplates killing the snake—there is a loaded British Webley revolver inside the trailer—but then makes a striking statement: "It is my duty as a park ranger to protect, preserve and defend all living things within the park boundaries, making no exceptions. Even if this were not the case I have personal convictions to uphold. Ideals, you might say. I prefer not to kill animals. I'm a humanist; I'd rather kill a man than a snake."

This is not as original a sentiment as it may sound. Decades earlier the poet Robinson Jeffers, who labelled himself an "anti-humanist," published a poem called "Hurt Hawks" that contained this sentiment: "I'd sooner, except the penalties, kill a man than a hawk." But in that instance Jeffers was euthanizing a crippled hawk that he'd been feeding for six weeks and had finally concluded had no hope of recovery. Abbey not only appropriated the shock value of Jeffers's verse, but turned it up a notch when he labelled it as a humanist sentiment rather than that of an anti-humanist.

---

† "Horny rattler" may have been a local common name for *Crotalus concolor*. The adults average about 60 centimeters (24 inches) in length, but its venom is among the most potent of all pit vipers in North America.

Abbey herded the rattlesnake away from his cabin with a shovel, and later, during a trip to the garbage dump, captured a gopher snake that he brought home to live under the trailer. He was an astute enough naturalist to realize that the gopher snake might protect him from rattlesnakes by competing for the same resources. People who live remotely in high desert biomes, however, prefer to host kingsnakes under their cabins because they prey upon rattlesnakes.

There are a number of times throughout the book where Abbey seems to delight in shocking the reader. Most notably, in the following chapter, "Cliffrose and Bayonets," he tells a story of young cottontail rabbit that he surprises while out in the desert. The rabbit freezes under a bush, its ears back, watching Abbey with "one bright eye." It occurs to Abbey to conduct an experiment, asking himself the question of what he'd do if this were a survival situation where he was starving and did not have a weapon. Abbey builds a bit of writerly suspense with this paragraph:

> There are a few stones scattered along the trail. I pick up one that fits well in the hand, that seems to have the optimum feel and heft. I stare at the cottontail hunched in his illusory shelter under the bush. Blackbrush, I observe, the common variety, sprinkled with tightly rolled little green buds, ready to burst into bloom on short notice. Should I give the rabbit a sporting chance, that is, jump it again, try to hit it on the run? Or brain the little bastard where he is?

Deciding that he's not a sportsman, he writes, "I rear back and throw the stone with all I've got straight at his furry head." What follows is one of the most outrageous passages in the book: "To my amazement the stone flies true (as if guided by a Higher Power) and knocks the cottontail head over tincups, clear out from under the budding blackbush. He crumples, there's the usual gushing of blood, etc., a brief spasm, and then no more. The wicked rabbit is dead."

If we can believe the text, Abbey astounds even himself, at least for a moment. Leaving the rabbit for the vultures, since it may have been infected with tularemia, he moves away, writing, "I continue my walk with a new, augmented cheerfulness which is hard to understand but is unmistakable." He decides that his experiment was a complete success, and that it would never be necessary to perform it again.

Much has been written by ecocritics and animal lovers wondering how Abbey can be considered an environmentalist after conducting such an experiment. But this is exactly the sort of debate the author hoped to stimulate. He wanted to burst the mold that defined an environmentalist, to make a place within the discourse for those who were not conventional nature lovers, at least not along the lines of John Muir or Aldo Leopold. There had to be room at the table for those who were not only angry but also even a bit wild. There had to be room for those who, like Abbey, refused to play by the rules.

We arrive at the rhetorical heart of *Desert Solitaire* in the next chapter, "Polemic: Industrial Tourism and the National Parks," and it is indeed a polemic, albeit one argued via narration. The story begins with how Abbey likes his job as a ranger, and even considers the $1.95-per-hour wage he earns to be generous, "I might even say munificent." The work is simple, Abbey explains, and it requires no mental effort. He gives a campfire talk on Saturday nights; the tourists leave on Sunday; and on Monday he empties the garbage cans, reads the discarded newspapers, sweeps out the outhouses, and cleans the Kleenex off the cactuses. He's off on Tuesday and Wednesday, usually spending his time in the "beer joints" of Moab, hanging out with uranium miners and cowboys. Then, on Thursdays he patrols the roads and trails, and on Fridays he inspects the campgrounds, hauls in firewood, and distributes toilet paper to the outhouses. It's an easy job, Abbey reflects, and he could see himself doing it forever except for one thing: progress, which he depicts as a small, dark cloud on the horizon, "no bigger than his hand."

Of course, this minimization doesn't fool the reader for a moment. The storyteller continues, "I was sitting out back on my 33,000-acre terrace, shoeless and shirtless, scratching my toes in the sand and sipping on a tall iced drink, watching the flow of evening over the desert." And what shows up, to our collective horror, arrives on a discordant note: "the snarling whine of a jeep in low range and four-wheel-drive, coming from an unexpected direction, from the vicinity of the old foot and horse trail that leads from Balanced Rock down toward Courthouse Wash and on to park headquarters near Moab." It was a gray jeep, covered with dust, with a government sticker on the side indicating it was from the Bureau of Public Roads.

This is the beginning of the end, as far as Abbey is concerned. In addition to two empty water bags flapping on the bumper, the jeep's contents were ominous: "Inside were three sunburned men in twill britches and engineering boots, and a pile of equipment: transit case, tripod, survey rod, bundles of wooden stakes. (Oh no!)"

As the engineers slake their thirst, Abbey learns that the government has decided to build a paved road to make it easier for tourists to access the backcountry.

Then we fast-forward into the future, written from a perspective several years later after the road was built and the flow of tourists grew from three thousand per year to three million. Abbey lists a slew of other national parks or monuments where similar development was taking place—Grand Canyon, Natural Bridges, Zion, and Capitol Reef among them—and tells us:

> I could easily cite ten more examples of unnecessary or destructive development for every one I've named so far. What has happened in these particular areas, which I chance to know a little and love too much, has happened, is happening, or will soon happen to the majority of our national parks and national forests, despite the illusory protection of the Wilderness Preservation Act, unless a great many citizens rear up on their hind legs and make vigorous political gestures demanding implementation of the Act.

Abbey goes on for pages railing against motorized tourists, "the indolent millions born on wheels and suckled on gasoline, who expect and demand paved highways to lead them in comfort, ease and safety into every nook and corner of the national parks." While parts of his diatribe are offensive by modern standards, especially in terms of park access for the elderly and disabled, much of what he wrote turns out to have been prescient when read in light of today's situation where the national parks are overwhelmed with tourism and choked with automobile traffic. Were Abbey alive today, he'd no doubt tell us that we've gotten exactly what we bargained for.

When the older, more politic, critically trained me rereads *Desert Solitaire*, I must remind myself of the hold the tome had on me when I first read it fifty-some years ago. I had just completed my first year of college and read it during the summer when I was employed as a merit-badge counselor at a scout ranch in Colorado. The more wicked the book seemed, the more I identified with it. I spent four summers wearing a uniform the same color as the ranger's uniform Abbey wore, and despite my commitment to be trustworthy, loyal, courteous, kind, et cetera, there was something to Cactus Ed's swagger that captivated me. The book not only captured my attention but also held on to it; I went so far as to write a master's thesis about *Desert Solitaire* some years later. At this point, however, I find sections of the narrative to lack merit.

The chapters that follow the industrial tourism polemic tend to ramble a bit, even though they resemble a few of the chapters in Mary Austin's *Land of Little*

Rain in how they feature local characters living the lives of ranch hands or miners. For the most part, they retain their nonfiction demeanor, but one of the chapters, "The Moon-Eyed Horse," is completely fiction, a short story Abbey had originally written independently of *Desert Solitaire*. It is not presented, however, as being of a different genre than the other chapters, a fact that has perplexed some critics and bothered others. One critic, Jerry Herndon, has suggested that the horse featured in the story may be an allegorical representation of Abbey himself.

The story begins with Abbey and a cowboy friend stopping in a canyon to water their horses. Abbey notices the tracks of a large, unshod horse, and brings them to his companion's attention. The companion tells Abbey that the tracks belong to a gelding that belongs to no one and is very shy and has been up in the canyon alone for ten years. This disturbs Abbey, who explains, "The horse is a gregarious beast, a herd animal, like the cow, like the human. It's not natural for a horse to live alone." So one month later Abbey decides to rescue the horse, making it his own. He chooses an unbearably hot day to head back up the canyon, but finally hears the horse breathing. He tempts it verbally while approaching it slowly, pausing after each step: "How long since you've stuck that ugly face of yours into a bucket of barley and bran? Remember what alfalfa tastes like, old pardner? How about grass, Moon-Eye? Green sweet fresh succulent grass, Moon-Eye, what do you think of that, eh?"

Abbey's "sermon," as he calls it, continues for many pages. At one point, he asks the horse whether it wants to die alone out in this canyon, only to be eaten by turkey vultures. To have his desiccated skeleton discovered by some miner when only the ribcage remained. This one-sided conversation goes on for hours, Abbey writing that it finally got to where he speaks one sentence and then waits ten minutes before the next argument occurs to him. Through it all, however, the horse refuses to rejoin society. In the end, as the sun sets, Abbey walks away, writing, "Once, twice, I thought I heard footsteps following me but when I looked back I saw nothing."

I doubt that this chapter could ever have stood on its own as an independent short story. Despite its realism, it would have seemed too contrived to work as fiction. The best possibility for it to have worked under the banner of nonfiction is if the reader ended up thinking, "I can't believe that Abbey went through all this to rescue an animal that didn't want to be rescued." In other words, the joke would have been on Abbey, but only if we believed that the incident really took place. Once we discover that the author did not indeed go through what the story claims to have occurred, never preaching a long sermon to a horse that wanted nothing to do with salvation, the farcical nature of the story causes it to unravel. To my mind, as an author myself who is concerned about readers trusting my veracity, it's disappointing that this story was presented as nonfiction because it forces me to wonder what other elements of *Desert Solitaire* never happened. Did Abbey not really kill that rabbit with a well-aimed rock? Did he really pull up the surveyor's stakes after they'd mapped out a road? Did he really have the ill-mannered conversations with tourists that he claims to have had?

What doesn't unravel, at least for me, is the quality of the prose. I have a digital copy of *Desert Solitaire*'s typed manuscript, each page containing dozens of edits and revisions, and it's clear that the author paid close attention to the writing, especially in terms of his descriptions of the landscape. He seemed to have been concerned above all with the flow of paragraphs, adding and subtracting paragraph breaks laboriously on almost every page.

One of the chapters where Abbey's wordsmithing is most apparent is "Water," a chapter that doesn't take the form of a story but is structured rather as a collection of observations, some meteorological, others descriptive of natural history. This is a chapter that could only have been written by someone who had spent a good deal of time hiking in the desert during its hotter, more arid seasons. Even if some of the lore presented here was not experienced by the author firsthand, he obviously did his homework regarding such phenomena as flash floods and quicksand. I remember distinctly the first time I experienced quicksand, remembering what Abbey had written and how accurately he described the experience: how the quicksand would not pull me down, but at the same time would not want to let me go if I stopped moving forward. My quicksand travail was on a beach on the Colorado River, just below a hot-spring waterfall where I'd thought it might be fun to take a shower, and as soon as I got back to my kayak, a bit shaken, I remember thinking, "Wow, that's just how Abbey said it would be."

Similarly, the chapter "Havasu" has always struck fear into my heart, and to this day I can't read it without getting sweaty palms. The story is set during a road trip to Los Angeles where Abbey "was riding with some friends from the University of New Mexico," so this probably occurred during the time when Abbey was a graduate student there, prior to his summers as a ranger at Arches. In the first paragraph we read, "On the way we stopped off briefly to roll an old tire into the Grand Canyon. While watching the tire bounce over tall pine trees, tear hell out of a mule train and disappear with a final grand leap into the inner gorge, I overheard the park ranger standing nearby say a few words about a place called Havasu, or

Havasupai." We can only wonder why the park ranger had nothing to say about the vandalism associated with the tire, but at this point in *Desert Solitaire*, in the thirteenth of eighteen chapters, many readers will have learned to take Cactus Ed with a grain of salt when he's waxing outrageous.

So Abbey decided to leave behind his friends and spend a month or two in Havasu, not living among the Supai tribe but living near them. Toward the end of that sojourn, he was out hiking alone, exploring a side canyon, when he realized late in the afternoon that he would not get back to his camp before dark unless he found a shortcut. This is where Abbey made a mistake that could easily have ended his life: "Nearby was another little side canyon which appeared to lead down into Havasu Canyon. It was a steep, shadowy, extremely narrow defile with the usual meandering course and overhanging walls; from where I stood, near its head, I could not tell if the route was feasible all the way down to the floor of the main canyon. I had no rope with me—only my walking stick. But I was hungry and thirsty, as always. I started down."

As Abbey descended the canyon, it turned to slickrock with cascades of small pools that still contained water from the last rain. These cascades grew in size until he got to one with a twelve-foot overhang. Although he knew that the sensible thing was to turn back, he dropped feet-first into the pool, hitting the bottom hard but without injury. He dog-paddled to the lip and was horrified to see that he wasn't as near the bottom as he'd hoped; the next overhanging cliff led to a rock rubble eighty feet below. At this point, he considered writing out his epitaph, not thinking he could climb back up to the higher pool.

Well, Abbey made it back up the slickrock, barely, climbing barefoot after his boots caused a fall on his first attempt. The story ends in the rain and the dark, where Abbey crawled into a coyote den and built a fire of twigs, using matches sealed in paraffin. He ends the story thus: "I stretched out in the coyote den, pillowed my head on my arm and suffered through the long long night, wet, cold, aching, hungry, wretched, dreaming claustrophobic nightmares. It was one of the happiest nights of my life."

One gets a sense, reading the later chapters in *Desert Solitaire*, that Abbey may have been fishing around for narratives to fill out his book. After "Havasu" comes "The Dead Man at Grandview Point," the tale of searching for a tourist lost out in the desert and then carrying his body back to civilization on a stretcher. "Tukuhnikivats, the Island in the Desert" follows, a narration about a desert mountain Abbey climbed solo, and then "Episodes and Visions," which once again ridicules the tourists who attended Abbey's weekend campfire talks, a chapter whose main point seems to be to offend Mormons, Catholics, Baptists, and Jews, roughly in that order.

While reading "Episodes and Visions" in preparation for this study, I found myself wondering whether I would be comfortable teaching this material for an undergraduate class on environmental literature. The last time I taught any of *Desert Solitaire*, I'd used a course reader that only included two chapters, "Cliffrose and Bayonets" and "Polemic: Industrial Tourism and the National Parks." At this juncture I'm not sure I'd want to invest class time in anything from the last hundred pages of the book, not only because of their lack of depth but also because they are increasingly offensive. We had read the complete book in a long-ago graduate seminar where we were interested in how Abbey engaged in a rhetoric of provocation. I don't remember anyone being offended by the prose, but these are different times and Abbey's irreverence, his political incorrectness, his sexism, and his xenophobia toward immigrants could prove problematic in today's classroom climate, at least to the point where it would need to be dealt with. In this regard, Abbey's writing has not aged as well as the works of earlier writers examined in this study.

That said, Abbey changed environmental discourse forever. It grew critical of social structure in new ways, becoming countercultural in a fashion that earlier environmentalists, such as Aldo Leopold and Rachel Carson, could never have imagined. In subsequent books, especially the novel titled *The Monkeywrench Gang*, Abbey laid the foundation for a type of environmental activism that became the hallmark of organizations such as Earth First, espousing a radical, eco-warrior approach to defending the environment "by any means necessary."

Edward Paul Abbey died in 1989. At his request, his body was transported in the bed of a pickup truck and buried in an old sleeping bag on public land in the Cabeza Prieta Desert in Arizona. He had instructed his friends to disregard all state laws regarding burial.

Pilgrim at Tinker Creek by Annie Dillard (1974)

Our life is a faint tracing on the surface of mystery, like the idle curved tunnels of leaf miners on the face of a leaf. We must somehow take a wider view, look at the whole landscape, really see it, and describe what's going on here. —FROM THE CHAPTER, "HEAVEN AND EARTH IN JEST"

In 1945, nuclear weapons were used twice in warfare, World War II came to a conclusion, Franklin D. Roosevelt was sworn in for a fourth term as U.S. president, dying that same year, the United Nations Charter was signed, a B-25 bomber crashed into the Empire State Building, and George Orwell's dystopian novel, *Animal Farm*, was published. The first ballpoint pens went on sale at the Gimbels Department Store in New York City that year, and Annie Dillard was born in Pittsburgh, Pennsylvania.

According to an unpublished biography written by Dillard's husband, Bob Richardson, she was an active child growing up in Pittsburgh: riding her bike everywhere, sledding so fast she broke her nose two days in succession, throwing a baseball at a strike zone painted in red on the garage door, and playing boogie-woogie on the piano. She went to the Ellis School, an independent all-girl's school, where the headmistress advised Dillard's parents that she should attend a southern college in order to smooth off her rough edges. In her autobiography, *An American Childhood*, Dillard would write: "I had hopes for my rough edges. I wanted to use them as a can opener, to cut myself a hole in the world's surface and exit through it."

Dillard attended Hollins College in Roanoke, Virginia, where she studied literature, theology, and creative writing. She fell in love with a creative writing professor, Richard Dillard, and by Christmas of her sophomore year was engaged to him. As her second husband, Richardson, tells the story: "At twenty she was a faculty wife; she finished her BA and an MA, played softball and pinochle, and taught herself to read topographical maps. She hiked and camped on the Appalachian trail and along the Blue Ridge Parkway. Mostly, however, she read and lesserly wrote poetry. She and her husband lived in a quiet suburban development in Roanoke, their back yard sloping sharply to an unremarkable stream, perhaps seventeen feet wide at its widest, called Tinker Creek."

Pilgrim at Tinker Creek (hereafter *Pilgrim*) was not her first book—it was one of two debut volumes Dillard published in 1974, the first of which was a poetry collection titled *Tickets for a Prayer Wheel*. The second book, a work of narrative nonfiction published two months later, won a Pulitzer Prize and was excerpted in *Harper's Magazine*, *Atlantic Monthly*, and *Sports Illustrated*. The reviews were not all positive, however. According to the Richardson biography, "*Kirkus Reviews* bombed it while it was still in galleys. Loren Eisely bombed it. Wendell Berry said it proposed no land-use ethic whatsoever. C. P. Snow was appalled. Eudora Welty wrote a long piece for the *New York Times Book Review* faulting the book for its undeveloped characters, its abstractions, and its bookishness."

To venture into *Pilgrim* is to trek the author's mind, unfettered and yet not completely wild, as she delves into the labyrinth of her own twenty-something consciousness. A sentence may follow the logic of the one that preceded it, or it might not, as in this short paragraph: "The wood duck flew away. I only caught a glimpse of something like a bright torpedo that blasted the leaves where it flew. Back at the house, I ate a bowl of oatmeal; much later in the day came a long slant of light that means good walking."

Although there were certainly critics who were appalled by the writing, others delighted in it. The same spectrum of reactions was felt by nature writers. Some, Dillard included, were not even certain it could be called "nature writing." However, a sizable number of nature writers, and I include myself in this group, found *Pilgrim* as freeing as it was uplifting. After Dillard, the divide between nature and culture was shattered.

Although many writers within the nature-writing genre had written in the first person, in *Pilgrim* the point of view rose to new heights. Take, for example, the first few sentences of the fourth chapter, "The Fixed," where the point of view takes precedence over the object being viewed: "I have just learned to see praying mantis egg cases. Suddenly I see them everywhere; a tan oval of light catches my eye, or I notice a blob of thickness in a patch of slender weeds. As I write I can see the one I tied to the mock orange hedge outside my study window. It is over an inch long and shaped like a bell, or like the northern hemisphere of an egg cut through its equator."

Compare the above passage with a typical observation in *Walden*: "A single gentle rain makes the grass many shades greener. So our prospects brighten on the influx of better thoughts. We should be blessed if we lived in the present always, and took advantage of every accident that befell us, like the grass which confesses the influence of the slightest dew that falls on it." Thoreau's observation is quickly transcended by a moral application. If there's a moral accompanying Dillard's observations, it's often about the discovery of nature's perversity. For example, after a multipage description of praying mantis reproduction, including the fact that the female eats the male's head during coitus, Dillard concludes, "Fish gotta swim and bird gotta fly; insects, it seems, gotta do one horrible thing after another. I never ask why of a vulture, or shark, but I ask why of almost every insect I see. More than one insect—the possibility of fertile reproduction—is an assault on all human value, all hope of a reasonable god."

She is clearly interrogating a different construct of nature than Thoreau was.

Dillard was intimately familiar with Thoreau's writing, having written a master's thesis, *Walden Pond and Thoreau*, where she argued that the pond itself served as "the central image and focal point for Thoreau's narrative movement between heaven and earth." In like manner, it could be said that Tinker Creek serves as the central image and focal point for Dillard's narrative movement between seeing perceptively and developing a sense of wonder.

If there is a fundamental difference in the transcendental nature of Thoreau's and Dillard's musings, it is in Dillard's occasional irreverence and the humor she finds within it. She can suggest, "We have brass candlesticks in our houses now; we ought to display praying mantises in our churches." On the very next page she will complain: "Nature is, above all, profligate. Don't believe them when they tell you how economical and thrifty nature is, whose leaves return to the soil. Wouldn't it be cheaper to leave them on the tree in the first place? This deciduous business alone is a radical scheme, the brainchild of a deranged manic-depressive with limitless capital. Extravagance! Nature will try anything once."

Back to Dillard's master's thesis, she seemed even then to understand where and how she might deviate from Thoreau's approach. She wrote, "The social satire in *Walden* is scattered in bits and pieces, never sustained or directed." Such is not the same in Dillard's writing.

At the beginning of chapter 5, "Untying the Knot," she finds a snakeskin out in the woods by the quarry, "lying in a heap of leaves right next to an aquarium someone had thrown away. I don't know why that someone hauled the aquarium deep into the woods to get rid of it; it had only one broken glass side." Yes, why on earth, we have to agree, would someone haul an aquarium with a broken side deep into the woods to get rid of it? Of course, Dillard takes the irony a step further, pointing out that it *only* had one broken glass side, as if an aquarium could still to be useful with such a minor defect.

These quips are almost throwaways, a sarcastic one-liner here and there, just often enough to bushwack the reader, here in a book that purports to be about its author developing a deeper sense of wonder. But this is precisely what gives *Pilgrim* its unique edge: Dillard catalogues the absurdity of the human experiment through such observations, but at the same time is making a case that transcendence is not only possible, but immanent.

Technically, what Dillard wrote in *Pilgrim* should probably not be considered satire simply because the writing is postmodern, and there's a difference between postmodern writing and satire. While both rely heavily on detecting the absurd, satire tends to be didactic—trying to teach a moral of some sort—while postmodern writing accepts absurdity as being an inevitable element of living in a world that is de facto ludicrous. We acknowledge that we live in a world where people drag broken aquariums deep into the woods. This is our world—but it's also a world where a snake uses the sharp edges of broken aquarium glass to help molt its skin.

When Dillard first examined the shed skin, it seemed to be tied in an eternal knot, at which point she realized the molt as a metaphor for seasonal change, noting that "there is a bit of every season in each season." This realization makes it impossible for Dillard, despite her impulse to do so, "to stick a net into time and say, 'Now,'" at the moment spring arrives, "just as men plant flags on the ice and snow and say, 'Here.'" Our postmodern nature writer, perhaps the first such among us, concludes, "But it occurred to me that I could no more catch spring by the tip of the tail than I could untie the apparent knot in the snakeskin; there are no edges to grasp. Both are continuous loops."

Despite this realization, Dillard portrays spring brilliantly in her descriptions, as this paragraph demonstrates: "The morning woods were utterly new. A strong yellow light pooled between the trees; my shadow appeared and vanished on the path, since a third of the trees I walked under were still bare, a third spread a luminous haze wherever they grew, and another third blocked the sun with new, whole leaves. The snakes were out—I saw a bright, smashed one on the path—and the butterflies were vaulting and furling about: the phlox was at its peak, and even the evergreens looked greener, newly created and washed."

There is something creative and playful in the above passage, but to me the paragraph doesn't demonstrate a new way of writing nature so much as it points us toward a new way of seeing it. Gone is the quasi-scientific approach to describing natural history that was handed down to us ever since Gilbert White, the English parson-naturalist, set the original bar in 1798 with *The Natural History and Antiquities of Selborne*. There is especially no attempt to be accurate in how the butterflies are vaulting and furling about. Gone is the moral compass that Ralph Waldo Emerson and Henry David Thoreau searched for in nature; the greener, newly created, and washed evergreens are a function of spring, not a signifier of divinity. Gone is the environmentalism of Aldo Leopold and Rachel Carson; the smashed snake is just a smashed snake. Dillard sees new life through the same lens she uses to see death, and it all works together to create a profound portrait.

Dillard seems inspired by the more wondrous aspects of natural history, such as the fact that "a newt can scent its home from as far as eight miles away." After delving into organismal minutiae for a page or two, she always returns to narrative. In this case, she reports that she was camping "alone" in a park in the Allegheny Mountains, and she spent the greater part of an afternoon watching children and newts. The newts outnumbered the children greatly, but the children seemed to be getting the best of the newts. One child was collecting them in a thermos mug to take home to feed an ailing cayman. Others, Dillard reports, "ran to their mothers with squirming fistfuls." One boy "was mistreating the newts spectacularly," throwing them at a shoreline stone. Diller tried to reason with this boy but tells us that nothing worked. Finally, the boy asked her whether a newt was male, and "in a fit of inspiration" she told the boy that it was a baby. He cried, "Oh, isn't he cute!" and then returned the newt carefully to the water.

The narrative of the children and the newts is not presented as a parable. It is, rather, a report from the field: observations of a naturalist who had intended, unsuccessfully, to camp out alone. We can do what we want with the story: it is up to the reader to find it either amusing, disgusting, or something else. Dillard is not advocating that we take action; she just wants us to know that this is part of the natural history of the newts she had been writing about in her "Spring" chapter.

Dillard then turns to trees, which she thinks "especially seem to bespeak a generosity of spirit. She quotes a line from the English philosopher and poet John

Cowper Powys, who said, "We have no reason for denying to the world of plants a certain slow, dim, vague, large, leisurely semiconsciousness," and she comments that "he may not be right, but I like his adjectives."

This is where Annie Dillard appeals to my sense of whimsy. On the surface, the whimsy may seem excessive: *should we not care whether Powys was right or wrong?* But we should harken back to something Dillard stated in a previous chapter, "Seeing." "Seeing is of course very much a matter of verbalization. Unless I call my attention to what passes before my eyes, I simply won't see it." In essence, in stating that she likes Powys's adjectives, Dillard is acknowledging that verbalization is as much a part of how he sees trees as it is a part of her observational process. She has stated, "Like a blind man at a ball game, I need a radio." The metaphorical radio she needs to comprehend nature is words, and this is all she can use to convey nature to the reader. The act of seeing is not distinct from the process of articulating what has been seen.

For those of us enamored with Dillard's writing, we not only like her adjectives, but her verbs as well. A close reading of the following paragraph proves the point:

On my way home, every bird I saw had something in its mouth. A male English sparrow, his mouth stuffed, was hopping in and out of an old nest in a bare tree, and sloshing around in its bottom. A robin on red alert in the grass, trailing half a worm from its bill, bobbed three steps and straightened up, performing unawares the universal robin trick. A mockingbird flew by with a red berry in its beak; the berry flashed in the sun and glowed like a coal from some forge or cauldron of the gods.

The adjectival phrases in this passage are sparse and perplexing. The nest is old. The tree is bare. The robin's alert is red, and the trick it performs is universal. The verbs are entirely spirited: the sparrow is both hopping and sloshing. The robin bobbed, straightened up, and performed. The berry flashed and glowed. There is a dynamism here that describes nature in terms of its animation. Every bird has something in its mouth, and there is a springtime urgency to the process of foraging. We do not need to be told that the nestlings are hungry—this is implicit in the descriptions of parental behavior.

Dillard's description of nature may often seem romantic, but is just as often the opposite. In May, for example, when she observes that "fullness is at its peak," she complains that the plants are closing in on her. "The neighborhood children are growing up; they aren't keeping all the paths open." As a solution, Dillard claims that she feels like buying them all motorbikes because "the woods are a clog of green." When she is finally up to her knees in honeysuckle, she beats a retreat to the duck pond.

Dillard will ultimately conclude, in her chapter "Stalking," that we "cannot study nature, per se, but only our own investigation of nature." She compares nature to a fan dancer whose fans can never be ripped away, making of it something intrinsically unknowable. It is a naturalist's lament: "The heron flaps away; the dragonfly departs at thirty miles an hour; the water strider vanishes under a screen of grass, the muskrat dives, and the ripples roll from the bank, flatten, and cease altogether." Her writing throughout the book reflects the fact that her knowledge of nature is cursory: she cannot tell us what it is, she can only describe her pursuit of it in and around Tinker Creek.

What is not cursory, to Dillard, is beauty, and Tinker Creek itself becomes a symbol of the beauty in nature. All she asks of the creek is that it surprise her, and she reports that it does "with each new drop." In a paragraph that starts "This Tinker Creek!" she waxes poetic: "These are the waters of beauty and mystery, issuing from a gap in the granite world; they fill the lodes in my cells with a light like petaled water, and they churn in my lungs mighty and frigid, like a big ship's screw."

To Dillard, this search for beauty takes precedence over the natural historian's desire to describe and catalogue. "What I aim to do is not so much learn the names of the shreds of creation that flourish in this valley, but to keep myself open to their meanings, which is to try to impress myself at all times with the fullest possible force of their very reality." While this could be interpreted as an ecological approach, one that concerns itself with the relation of each species to the next, "meaning" is a tricky term in Dillard's cosmos, one that doesn't imply any sort of teleology, any sense of creation having a design or purpose. She rejects any notion of a supreme being standing over evolution with a blue pencil to say, "Now that one, there, is absolutely ridiculous, and I won't have it." She understands that utility to the creature is evolution's only aesthetic consideration, and that this allows for certain absurdities. She explains, "Of the intricacy of form, I know some answers and not others: I know why the barbules on a feather hook together, and why the Henle's loop loops, but not why the elm tree's leaves zigzag, or why butterfly scales and pollen are shaped just so. But of the variety of form itself, of the multiplicity of forms, I know nothing."

And that, perhaps, is the aesthetic behind the multiplicity of forms.

Nowhere in the book does the absurdity of the natural world become as apparent as in the tenth chapter, "Fecundity." It is my favorite chapter in the book.

When Dillard claims to be appalled by the level of fecundity in the biotic world, she should be taken at her word. It is not hyperbole when she writes: "I don't know what it is about fecundity that so appalls. I suppose it is the teeming evidence that birth and growth, which we value, are ubiquitous and blind, that life itself is so astonishingly cheap, that nature is as careless as it is bountiful, and that with extravagance goes a crushing waste that will one day include our own cheap lives, Henle's loops and all. Every glistening egg is a memento mori." Dillard catalogues the fact that the barnacles encrusting a half mile of shoreline can exude a "million million larvae," hatched into the sea "in milky clouds." Then she asks, "What if God has the same affectionate disregard for us that we have for barnacles?"

As readers we should have seen this question coming. Dillard ponders whether there is a better way to run the universe, and then states, "Evolution loves death more than it loves you, or me. This is easy to write, easy to read, and hard to believe." She complains that she hoped her project to live by the side of a creek would help her shape her life to its free flow, but she now realizes that the creek might not be buoying her up but dragging her down instead. At the conclusion of the chapter on fecundity, she writes: "The world has signed a pact with the devil; it had to. It is a covenant to which everything, even every hydrogen atom, is bound. The terms are clear: if you want to live, you have to die; you cannot have mountains and creeks without space, and space is a beauty married to a blind man."

Not one to remain in a reflective funk, Dillard shakes off her doldrums in the first paragraph of the next chapter, "Stalking," where she writes, "Summer: I go down to the creek again, and lead a creek life. I watch and stalk."

We must ask here why watching and stalking are elements of a creek life. Five chapters earlier, she had reflected that watching the creek upstream was an uplifting process of looking toward the future, the flow that is forthcoming. She went so far as to say, "There must be something wrong with a creekside person who, all things being equal, chooses to face downstream. It's like fouling your own nest." And now we are told that learning to stalk muskrats took Dillard several years. First, she had to learn where the muskrats hung out on the creek, and then she had to learn not to walk on the banks to find them, but rather to wait on a bridge, perfectly still, watching upstream in the cool of the evening. But this process of stalking is worth the while. Dillard writes, "The great hurrah about wild animals is that they exist at all, and the greater hurrah is the actual moment of seeing them. Because they have a nice dignity, and prefer to have nothing to do with me, not even as the simple objects of my vision. They show me by their very wariness what a prize it is simply to open my eyes and behold."

More than anything, I suspect that what Dillard defines as "creek life" was the process of leaving suburbia behind, if not as a locus for her explorations, then at least as a narrative base for her interrogation of nature.* In terms of muskrats, Tinker Creek's apex predator, Dillard confesses that learning to observe them was a process of working patiently through mistakes to develop a pure form of skill, much like learning to pitch or play chess. She instructs us that "rarely is luck involved. I do it right or I do it wrong; the muskrat will tell me, and that right early." But Dillard explains that the creek life has its rewards, "Living this way by the creek, where the light appears and vanishes on the water, where muskrats surface and dive, and redwings scatter,† I have come to know a special side of nature." She describes this as the natural world's "touch-and-go" side, where nature, after flashing a come-hither look, "drops the handkerchief, turns tail, and is gone."

Dillard seems most intrigued with nature when it surprises her, when it performs contrary to her expectations, and when it seems so to defy logic far enough to become ridiculous or absurd. She appreciates it when, in her words, "nature seems to catch you by the tail." One such event, near dusk, was when she was sitting on a flat rock, watching a copperhead snake four feet away, a snake that had been lying on the rock unmoved for hours. While Dillard watched, a mosquito sang in her ear, and she waved it away. Then the mosquito landed on her ankle, and she brushed it off. The mosquito, to her utter disbelief, lighted on the copperhead. For two or three full minutes, which Dillard reports seemed like an hour, it sucked the snake's blood, but the snake never moved. She completes this narrative, "I looked at the snake; I looked beyond the snake to the ragged chomp on the hillside where years before men had quarried stone; I rose, brushed myself off, and walked home."

---

* In a 2015 article, "The Thoreau of the Suburbs," in *The Atlantic* by Diana Saverin, Dillard is quoted thus: "I didn't say, 'I walked by the suburban brick houses.' Why would I say that to the reader? But when I saw that reviewers were acting like it was the wilderness, I said, 'Oh, shit.'"

† It's possible that this is a common name she uses for red-winged blackbirds, *Agelaius phoeniceus*. In ornithological circles, the term "redwing" is more properly ascribed to *Turdus iliacus*, a Eurasian thrush.

Dillard uses the word "chomp" or "chomped" eight times throughout *Pilgrim*, but it's always a verb except in the above sentence where the chomp is the metaphorical bite taken out of a hillside by human industry. This is social commentary, Dillard style.

When the book first came out, she was criticized repeatedly because *Pilgrim* didn't contain the same sort of social commentary found in *Walden*, but I think that such criticism is unfair. While Dillard, a Thoreau scholar, placed her book squarely in the tradition of *Walden*, going so far as to name her goldfish after Thoreau's best friend, Ellery Channing, she chose a distinctly different substrate upon which to base her reflections. Where Thoreau had his placid pond, Dillard has her dynamic creek. Likewise, where Thoreau's project was to simplify, Dillard's seems to have been to embrace complexities. This may be Dillard's ultimate contribution to literary natural history, giving us permission to embrace complexities when attending to and describing the natural world.

There was no dearth of social disquiet when *Pilgrim* was published in 1974. The Watergate hearings were underway, three articles of impeachment had been drafted for the president of the United States, and the war in Vietnam was drawing to an inglorious close. Dillard, however, chooses not to engage in society's troubles; not only are there others taking up those crusades, but she seems to understand that her concerns are outside the greater social agenda. In the chapter, "Intricacy," she writes:

> I have often noticed that these things, which obsess me, neither bother nor impress other people even slightly. I am horribly apt to approach some innocent at a gathering and, like the ancient mariner, fix him with a wild, glitt'ring eye and say, "Do you know that in the head of the caterpillar of the ordinary goat moth there are two hundred twenty-eight separate muscles?" The poor wretch flees. I am not making chatter; I mean to change his life. I seem to possess an organ that others lack, a sort of trivia machine.

I have to believe that if Thoreau had been a contemporary of Dillard and had been schooled in postmodern sensitivities, he would have enjoyed Dillard's reflections enormously. He wrote, after all: "If a man does not keep pace with his companions, perhaps it is because he hears a different drummer. Let him step to the music which he hears, however measured or far away." This was radical thinking in his day and was exactly the sort of thinking that gave Dillard a good reason not to become the next Thoreau.

Thoreau saw the order in nature and wrote about it with insightful dispassion. Dillard saw the disorder in nature and wrote about it with passionate insights that were altogether divergent from anything that had been written before. She shared some of Thoreau's passions, however, including an affinity for wild creatures, but with a different emphasis: Thoreau wrote about a mouse that would join him for meals because it had learned that there would be crumbs it could forage; Dillard wrote about the fact that 10 percent of all the world's species are parasitic insects. Thoreau's essay, "Walking," opens with the phrase, "I want to speak a word for Nature." He writes his essay as nature's advocate, a champion on behalf of the freedom and wildness that can be found in nature. In *Pilgrim*, Dillard takes an opposite approach. Instead of nature's champion, she affects the role of a tattletale, the one who writes to expose nature's absurdities. We must ask why. Why is it important to know that mosquitos suck the blood of venomous snakes; that giant water bugs can eviscerate a frog by injecting an enzyme that dissolves the victim's muscles, bones, and organs; and why is it important to know that "large spiders in barns have been known to trap, wrap, and suck hummingbirds"?

To answer that question, I suggest we take the author at her word. In the final chapter of *Pilgrim at Tinker Creek*, Dillard writes two of the most astonishing sentences in the book: "We are people; we are permitted to have dealings with the creator and we must speak up for the creation. God *look* at what you've done to this creature, look at the sorrow, the cruelty and the long damned waste!" The best strategy at this point is for the reader to take a breath, and then ask, "Is this possible?" *Is it possible that the book wasn't actually written for us, the human readers, but for God, the creator of all this nature?* And the critic must ask whether it is possible that, rather than being a theodicy, the book is a prayer to an unknown god, a prayer that exclaims, "I don't get it! I may love it, but I don't understand it."

But we should remember that Dillard's book-long prayer is also about beauty, something she very much understands.

I have a few copies of *Pilgrim at Tinker Creek*, just as I have multiple copies of *Walden*, *Sand County Almanac*, *Silent Spring*, and *Desert Solitaire*, books I've discussed with many of my classes. My best copy of *Pilgrim* is leather-bound, embossed with gold filigree, has gilt pages, and is signed by the author. It was a bit pricier than the leather-bound Bible that was gifted to me as a college student, but that scripture doesn't contain author signatures and was never awarded a Pulitzer Prize. I was hesitant about underlining in the leather-bound copy, at least at first, but some of the sentences are so precious that they just had to be underscored.

A good book is one that you can read a decade later, and then another decade after that, and still be startled by something you'd never noticed before. *Pilgrim at Tinker Creek* is such a book for me. It continues to be instructive, and it unfolds in new layers that I'd missed during previous readings.

Refuge: An Unnatural History of Family and Place by Terry Tempest Williams (1991)

After dinner, we would spread out our sleeping bags in a circle, heads pointing to the center like a covey of quail, and watch the Great Basin sky fill with stars. Our attachment to the land was our attachment to each other. —FROM THE CHAPTER, "BURROWING OWLS"

In 1955, Disneyland opened in California, the Johnny Carson Show debuted on television, the minimum wage in the United States was raised to $1.00 per hour, and the Salk polio vaccine was deemed safe and effective. Rosa Parks was arrested for refusing to give up her seat on a bus, and Dr. Martin Luther King led a bus boycott in Montgomery, Alabama. That same year the "Teapot" series of above-ground nuclear tests was conducted at the Nevada Test Site, the USS Nautilus became the first operational nuclear submarine, and the United States became involved in a war in Vietnam. *Lolita* was published by Vladimir Nabokov, Albert Einstein died and Terry Tempest Williams was born.

I met Williams at an early point in my teaching career, when she did a two-week writer's residency at an all-girls boarding school where I was a member of the faculty. This was soon after *Refuge* was published when her career was just taking off. She visited my classes one day, leading discussions of the essay appended to *Refuge*, "The Clan of One-Breasted Women." My students seemed intrigued by the title when I assigned it—word quickly went out that "we're reading about breasts in Farnsy's class!"—and I had no doubt the essay would be perused comprehensively by the time our guest author arrived. Students came to class prepared, and our guest mesmerized them with the narrative of how nuclear fallout had ravaged her family.

My first reading of *Refuge* took place before I was a card-carrying birder. At that point, I was only familiar with half the birds Williams included in the book, but I appreciated it anyway for its deep sense of place. During my most recent reading of the book, while I was preparing to write this chapter, I realized it was the first time I'd read *Refuge* since my cancer diagnosis several years ago. Then, early in the book, when Williams relates a phone call where her mother told her about a tumor that had been discovered, it chilled me to remember a similar conversation my mother had with me when her tumor was diagnosed. In its starkness, the sparse structure of Williams's sentences made them sound as if they were adjunct to my own memory: "She hung up. The dial tone returned. I listened to the line until it became clear that I had heard what I heard."

I found it difficult, a few pages later, to read about the day Williams's mother had surgery, when the family heard the news that the tumor was malignant and that the surgeons had not been able to get to it all. I reacted in ways that I don't recall from my first reading thirty years ago: I teared up. Let this be a trigger warning for anyone who has had a parent, spouse, close friend, or other family member go through the cancer experience: the "Whimbrels" chapter may be hard to read. It's a tough read for cancer patients as well; that said, I'm glad I read it again. But I had to put the book down at page thirty-nine and go for a walk. It helped that water was nearby.

Each chapter takes the name of a bird species, and most chapters integrate that bird's natural history into the narrative. Below the chapter title is a simple notation indicating Great Salt Lake's level. The first chapter starts with the lake at 4,204.7 feet and progresses through when it is well above its flood level. I checked the lake's level the day I began writing this chapter, it was—and currently is—in the throes of what's been called a "thousand-year drought," and it was at 4,188.63 feet. While this is only a difference of 16.04 feet, one should remember that the average depth of the lake is fourteen feet, and its maximum depth is 35 feet. In terms of surface area, the lake that covered some 3,000 square miles when Williams was writing about it, currently only fills 950 square miles with water. While much of this can be attributed to drought, it must also be observed that 3.3 billion liters of water—872 billion gallons—is diverted each year for both agricultural and residential purposes from the rivers and streams that normally fill the lake. Even if the drought ends tomorrow, it's unlikely that the lake will return to a level of 4,200 feet in my lifetime.

There is no mention in *Refuge* of climate change even though concerns about anthropomorphic global warming had already emerged within environmental writing by the time of the book's publication in 1991. Rather, *Refuge* focused on a historical event that took place in late May of 1983 when the massive snowpack in the Wasatch mountains melted. As Williams described it, "Yesterday's temperature was sixty-two degrees, Fahrenheit. Today it is ninety-two. All hell is about to break loose in the mountains. A quick thaw is a quick flood." During this historic flood, the Bear River Migratory Bird Refuge, from which the book gets its title, was inundated with water. In an apropos thesis statement for the book, Williams writes, "I could not separate the Bird Refuge from my family. Devastation respects no boundaries. The landscape of my childhood and the landscape of my family, two things I had always regarded as bedrock, were now subject to change. Quicksand."

Not every chapter is about trauma. "Peregrine Falcon," for example, is entirely about birds. We learn that during a Christmas Bird Count, Williams was assigned to the landfill. "The local Audubon hierarchy," Williams relates, "tell me I am sent here because I know gulls." The deeper truth, Williams confesses with delight, is that she is sent to the dump because they secretly know she likes it. It's not the gulls that most command her attention, however; it's the starlings, a bird that many birders hold in distain. Williams reflects, "Perhaps we project on to starlings that which we deplore in ourselves: our numbers, our aggression, our greed, and our cruelty. Like starlings, we are taking over the world." But for Williams the choreography of starling flocks takes her breath away. Without using the word, she describes their murmurations as "they wheel and turn, twist and glide, with no apparent leader."

It's not the starlings that ultimately hold her interest, however. "Suddenly, the flock pulls together like a winced eye, then opens in an explosion of feathers." A peregrine, it turns out, has taken its prize. Williams completes the chapter telling us that as she continues her count, it's the falcon that she waits for.

Refuge was written from the perspective of an adherent of the Mormon faith, a person proud to be a fifth-generation Mormon, a descendent of the original pioneers who settled Utah. Although William disaffiliated with her church in years subsequent to the publication of *Refuge*, that doesn't diminish the strong, familial spirituality that helped her deal with a mother dying of cancer and that oriented her toward finding the divine in the comings and goings of the natural world. There are a few places within the book where she is critical of Mormon history. For example, after describing cooperative fishing among American white pelicans, she compares their behavior to the cooperative communal lifestyle recommended by Brigham Young's United Order. She points out that the communes based on Young's vision began to crumble because "they were forgetting one critical component: diversity."

A few paragraphs later she sums up the social experiment by comparing it to the lived experience of *Pelecanus erythrorhynchos*: "Brigham Young's United Order wanted to be independent from the outside world. The Infinite Order of Pelicans suggests there is no such thing."

One of the difficulties of being a memoirist comes when delving into family history, especially recent history such as how a family deals with sickness and death. In a 1992 interview with Terry Gross on NPR's *Fresh Air*, Williams revealed that she gave family members an opportunity to edit the *Refuge* manuscript, in essence giving her family a veto over what parts of their experience would be included in the book. That in itself was a tremendous act of faith, faith that the family would understand that the author's stance, even when critical, was motivated by love and respect.

While the author's stance in *Refuge* is animated by faith and a love of place, it is driven equally by the environmental concern of a naturalist. This tends to be a background presence in the book for the first hundred pages but comes out strongly in the chapter, "Redheads," which catalogues the effects of Great Salt Lake's flooding on various species, especially avian species. Central to Williams's environmental concerns are those regarding wetlands, which she considers to be the most productive ecosystems on the planet as well as the most threatened. She notes that "California has lost ninety-five percent of its wetlands over the past one hundred years," while "eighty-five percent of Utah's wetlands have been lost in the last two." The paradox of this crisis in terms of the Great Basin is that its marshes were disappearing "naturally." She claims that in pre-development times the birds would "simply move up" whenever the lake levels, rose, but in the current flooding they were unable to because "they find themselves flush against freeways and a rapidly expanding airport."

Of the waterfowl, one of the species most susceptible to high water around the Great Salt Lake are redheads, *Aythya americana*. Williams quotes a waterfowl biologist who assessed that this duck population was down almost eighty percent due to the flooding; he predicted that it would take up to seven years after the lake receded before significant improvement could be seen, and up to twenty years for the population to rebound. Although the population did eventually recover somewhat, it never achieved levels prior to the flood of 1983, at which point the Great Salt Lake held the largest population of breeding redheads in North America, as well as the highest concentration of birds per wetland acre.

There is an interesting back-and-forth between themes of environmental loss and loss to cancer in the book's middle chapters. For example, the chapter immediately following "Redheads" is "Killdeer," a short chapter narrating a picnic near the lake when women from three generations—Williams, her mother, and a niece—examine each other's horoscopes. Of course, predictions regarding one's future can be a sensitive matter for a cancer patient, and the chapter includes a beautiful reflection about when William's mother asked her oncologist what she should plan for her future. The doctor replied that she should live each day as richly as she could. This was advice she took to heart even as she lay in bed after the doctor left, pondering such questions as whether she would live to see her children marry, or whether she would ever know the joy of holding her grandchildren. At the end of a long paragraph, Williams quotes her mother's words during the picnic, "For the first time in my life, I started to be fully present in the day I was living. I was alive. My goals were no longer long-range plans, they were daily goals much more meaningful to me because at the end of each day, I could evaluate what I had done." This is followed up by a short, one-sentence paragraph that reads: "A flock of sandpipers wheeled in front of us." Fifteen chapters later, a similar sentence will find its way into the narration of the family praying together immediately after her mother's death: "In the privacy of one another's company, we openly celebrated and grieved Mother's passing. A flock of sanderlings wheeling over the waves of grief."

The pattern of bird observations in much of the text marks the presence of nature in personal history, and yet these observations are not interpreted as signs or portents—their presence is real, not symbolic. The reader gets a sense that although the birds have a narrative purpose in both the cancer and refuge storylines, and, although their destiny is intertwined with humanity, they have a value intrinsic unto themselves.

During the first half of the book, Williams had been working as curator of education for the Utah Museum of Natural History, but, in the chapter "Roadrunner," we learn that she'd been promoted to a position as naturalist-in-residence, which meant she would spend more time in the field as well as have more time to write. This also meant that she could spend more time with her mother by involving her in field research. I noticed, from that point forward, a subtle change in the writing: it become a bit more edgy in terms of its orientation toward social justice, a bit less journalistic, and notably more "creative" along the lines of creative writing as a distinct practice. There is an opening up of form in that chapter, for example, in the inclusion of a ten-paragraph anecdote about Williams and her mother checking into a casino in Nevada for a night and being given complementary tickets for ten dollars' worth of nickels. They decided to try their hands at the slot machines, and both had a hot streak, although Williams became conservative with her wagers a moment too soon, missing out on what would have been a large jackpot. In that same chapter she includes, verbatim, a letter she'd received from her niece about how to locate Halley's Comet with her binoculars. This loosening up of the text, here in the middle of the book, works wonders for the book's energy, especially in terms of Williams arriving at her narrative voice. One gets the sense that this is the real Terry Tempest Williams, no longer an author constrained to produce the proper sort of composition that might generally be expected of a museum curator.

The following chapter, "Magpies," opens with the newly freed author telling us that the Mormon Church had declared Sunday, May 5, 1986, to be a day of prayer on behalf of the weather, prayers that the rains may be stopped. This short paragraph is followed by an even shorter one, all of three words, saying, "Monday, it rained." Then comes an obscure bit where Williams complains of being distracted by magpies and having hit rock bottom, none of which makes sense until she writes, still with a touch of obfuscation: "Today, I feel stronger, learning to live within the natural cycles of a day and to not expect so much from myself. As women, we hold the moon in our bellies. It is too much to ask to operate on full-moon energy three hundred and sixty-five days a year. I am in the crescent phase. And the energy we expend emotionally belongs to the hidden side of the moon."

The chapter winds along somewhat experimentally, and the reader learns in the end that "a deep sadness" washes over the author due to the continued rise of the lake. She concludes the chapter writing out her frustrations as the emergent activist she is soon to become: "There is no one to blame, nothing to fight. No developer with dreams of condominiums. No toxic waste dump than would threaten the birds. Not even a single dam on the Bear River to oppose. Only a simple natural phenomenon: the rise of Great Salt Lake."

A creative flair moves into Williams's natural history observations at this point as well, as can be found in a close reading of a paragraph from the "Long-Billed Curlews" chapter: "I watch two western grebes through my binoculars. Their eyes are rubies against white feathers. The male's black head-feathers are flared and flattened on top, so they resemble Grace Jones. The female is impressed as she swims alongside. All at once, they arch their backs, extend their necks, and dash across the flat water with great speed and grace. They sink back down. They rise up again, running across the water. They sink back down."

The first sentence in the above passage isn't really about the birds, it's about the author, watching through binoculars. This differentiates the writing from normal ornithological description, where the author tends to stay outside the picture. In the second sentence, rather than comparing the eyes to rubies, Williams states that they *are* rubies. While this may be technically incorrect from a scientific view, the writing is stronger when the simile is avoided. This is followed by a description of head plumage so that it resembles Grace Jones, a Jamaican new-wave singer whose cover of a 1981 studio album, *Nightclubbing*, featured a Jean-Paul Goude painting with Jones wearing an Armani suit and sporting a ultra-square flattop haircut, cigarette in mouth. Again, this sort of comparison would not be tolerated in most ornithological discourse. Neither would most scientific naturalists be comfortable stating that the female was impressed as she swam alongside the male, since that would impose on the bird a theory of mind about which we can never be certain. Then, at the end of the paragraph, Williams's writing turns to the lyrical as she describes the courtship ceremony known to ornithologists as "rushing." Not only does Williams engage in the description without resorting to ornithological jargon, but note here how she repeats an entire sentence, "They sink back down." This is not done as a rhetorical device, but rather gives a sense of the repetitious element of grebe courtship. In the end what we realize is that Williams, even when writing as a naturalist, eschews a conventional, ornithologically correct approach and yet is able to describe a specific avian behavior with considerable expertise, verbal artistry, and a light touch.

The deeper one gets into the book, the more overt its spirituality becomes. In the chapter "Long-billed Curlews," we find a reflection about the unnerving solitary nature of Williams's travels around the northern stretches of the lake. She states that she is never entirely at ease because she is aware of the lake's will, and that its mood can change in minutes. She reflects that, in the "throbbing silence of the Great Basin," she needs to keep tight reins on her imagination, stating, "The pearl-handed [SIC] pistol I carry in my car lends me no protection. Only the land's mercy and a calm mind can save my soul. And it is here I find grace." Williams understands how the desert turns people into believers, pointing out further, "If the desert is holy, it is only because it is a forgotten place that allows us to remember the sacred." Then after quoting a passage from the Mormon scripture, *Doctrine and Covenants*, that she always carries with her, she confesses that she prays to the birds:

> I pray to the birds.
>
> I pray to the birds because I believe they will carry the messages of my heart upward. I pray to them because I believe in their existence, the way

their songs begin and end each day—the invocations and benedictions
of Earth. I pray to the birds because they remind me of what I love rather
than what I fear. And at the end of my prayers, they teach me how to listen.

This oft-quoted passage has been put to music, printed on posters and
signed-by-the-author mementos, committed to memory, and recited as a public
prayer. While the opening sentence contains a theology that might challenge
mainstream Judeo-Christian orthodoxy, the passage concludes with two incon-
testable statements of fact, especially for birders. Williams's appraisal of birdsong
as "the invocations and benedictions of Earth" refocuses everything she will say
about birdsong throughout the rest of the memoir.

I use the term "memoir" here with some trepidation. While much of American nature writing contains autobiographical elements, these memoir-like bits
are usually anecdotal, and the subsequent writing does not confirm to memoir
as genre until fairly recently. It seems that what differentiates a work as memoir
is that the first-person narrative, based on personal memories, focuses on the
narrator overcoming an obstacle as a major element of the author's life history.
We shall see this exemplified in the final chapter of this study, which deals with a
book written in a classical memoir format, even to the point of identifying itself
as a memoir in the subtitle. In my opinion, where *Refuge* crosses into memoir as
genre is in the author dealing with her mother's impending death.

In the chapter, "Western Tanager," Williams narrates the visit with her
mother's oncologist where she opts out of an additional round of chemotherapy
after a new tumor has been found, this despite knowing that the tumor will
ultimately result in a blockage that will make her unable to eat. This becomes
a turning point, especially at a family dinner shortly thereafter where Diane
Tempest says, "It feels good to finally be able to embrace my cancer. It's almost
like a friend. For the first time I feel like moving with it and not resisting what is
ahead." For me, rereading this as a cancer patient more than four years after my
initial diagnosis, still technically in remission but realizing that my remission
would probably be ephemeral, this was the most difficult passage to read in the
entire memoir, especially when Williams's mother asks her to help her through
her death. Williams wrote, "I laid my head on her lap and closed my eyes. I could
not tell if it was my mother's fingers combing through my hair, or the wind."

I found this passage particularly poignant, affecting me much more than
it had upon my first reading at the age of thirty-seven. This realization caused

me to question, at least for a moment, whether my critique of this book lacks the necessary objectivity. While there is always a subjective element to literary analysis, the critique should move beyond the critic's personal history. There is no way around the fact that I am reading this memoir as a cancer survivor myself, as someone who has recently lost a mother to sarcoma, and who has recently lost a dear friend and colleague to metastatic breast cancer. I suspect that my medical and personal experience affects how I explicate the text in ways that would not parallel my appraisal of other works included in this study.

One more thing we learn in "Western Tanager" is that the Bear River Migratory Bird Refuge was abandoned by the US Fish and Wildlife Service, having been completely inundated by the rising lake. Throughout the next few chapters, the narrative comes in short blocks of text, often two or three paragraphs long, separated by section breaks. This happens both in chapters dealing with cancer and natural history, although, at this point in the narrative, the cancer story is taking precedence. The convergence of the two narratives creates a dynamic tension as time moves forward, and a suspense is created about inevitable outcomes. At one point, after her mother has gone through a second surgery to remove an intestinal blockage, Williams writes, "A person with cancer dies in increments, and a part of you slowly dies with them." This message can be seen not only in what the author writes but also how she structures her writing physically, especially in terms of section breaks—the gaps help relieve the strain as the cancer takes over and the refuge floods.

At just the point where the narrative tension seems that it can't get any more strained, Williams begins a new chapter with a sentence that seems to come from an entirely different storyline, "For ten days, I have done nothing but watch whales quietly surfacing, diving deep, and surfacing. The story has been transported, at least temporarily, to a quaint fishing village at the northern tip of Vancouver Island in British Columbia. The respite creates a bit of breathing room for the reader, but it only lasts for a couple pages. Then, abruptly, after a section break, Williams writes in the present tense, "I feel like I am floating in salt water, completely at the mercy of currents. Mimi [her paternal grandmother] was operated on this morning for breast cancer, September 8, 1986, my birthday." At that point, the narrative shifts between present and past tense with each section break until a final paragraph in the chapter where Williams seems to alight on the book's central theme: "I am slowly, painfully discovering that my refuge is not found in my mother, my grandmother, or even the birds of Bear River. My refuge exists in my capacity to love. If I can learn to love death, then I can begin to find refuge in change."

There have been numerous reflections on death at this point, and yet the concept of actually learning to love death comes as an eye-opener. Earlier, Williams had likened birth itself to our first death, at a point our umbilical cord is cut and the separation child from the mother's body is immediate. A few chapters later, she wrote of dealing with her denial about her mother's terminal diagnosis, writing how she refused to believe that her mother would die, "And by denying her cancer, even her death, I deny her life." Further on, when her mother had decided not to undergo a further round of chemotherapy, there was a dialogue about her mother learning to relinquish life by becoming an open vessel and letting life flow through, which Williams at first did not understand until her mother explained that it was not that she was giving up. "I am just going with it. It's as if I am moving into another channel of life that lets everything in. Suddenly, there is nothing more to fight."

What struck me most about the chapters dealing with the loss of Williams's mother is the contemporaneous nature of the writing. The text feels more as if we are reading from the author's daily journal, and this style adds to the intense personal nature of what is being shared with the readers. At times, it feels as if the writer is writing in the instant action is taking place. Even when the past tense is used, there is little time lag between the event and its written record. For example, Williams writes, "A week ago, Mother asked me to write her a story. Today, I read it to her."

More often, however, narration is recorded in the present tense, as in these excerpts:

- "I get up to wash my hands. In the mirror, I see my mother's face."
- "I cry out from my soul, burying my head in the quilt that covers her.
- "I feel my mother's hand gently stroking the top of my head."
- "I am home. Our power is out. Brooke is lighting candles. My brothers and I agree we will not return to the house. Our father is the one who needs to be with Mother when she goes."
- "It is the third day since Mother's death. A candle is lit. Let me begin."

Then, finally, in the chapter "Birds-of-Paradise," there is a switch back to the past tense: "Mother was buried yesterday."

It seems germane that in *Refuge*, a book much concerned with endings, the ending is not entirely satisfying. There is another death, Williams's grandmother. Great Salt Lake finally begins to recede, but the story doesn't feel over. In the final paragraphs, Williams and her husband take their canoe out into the Great Salt Lake and scatter marigold petals in her mother's memory. It could be theorized that the narrative isn't concluded until twenty-one years later with the publication of *When Women Were Birds: Fifty-Four Variations on Voice*, a book that has been called a love story Williams wrote to her mother.

Upon completing my recent perusal of the *Refuge*, I harkened back to the last paragraph of the book's prologue, where Williams concluded: "I have been in retreat, this story is my return." Note here that the story is not *about* the author's return, but that it is the vehicle of the return from whatever retreat she was on. We get the sense that Williams may have been writing less for the edification of the reader and more to assist with her own process of sorting out what happened to a refuge, a lake, and a family.

Refuge includes an epilogue, however, "The Clan of One-Breasted Women," previously mentioned as the text my class discussed with Williams many years ago. It is one part memoir, the other part manifesto, with an opening paragraph that in many ways tells the whole story: "I belong to a Clan of One-Breasted Women. My mother, my grandmothers, and six aunts have all had mastectomies. Seven are dead. The two who survive have just completed rounds of chemotherapy and radiation."

This epilogue as not about genetic or hereditary disease but about having lived in Utah downwind of the above-ground nuclear tests of the 1950s. The epilogue makes the case for her family's cancer being the result of atomic testing, and also documents Williams's entry into civil disobedience when she crossed the line of the Nevada Test Site with nine other Utah women. As a writer, my favorite line comes at the end of Williams narrative of being arrested, handcuffed, and frisked, when the officer found a pen and a pad of paper tucked inside her left boot. When the officer sternly asks, "What are these?" Williams answers with a single word. "Weapons."

These days, Williams considers herself to be a "citizen writer." By this she means that she speaks out on behalf of an ethical stance toward life. As her writing corpus has developed, she has become increasingly concerned with how environmental issues become issues of social justice, especially in terms of how our species exercises power over nonhuman species. As such, *Refuge: An Unnatural History of*

Family and Place serves as an entry into a protracted discourse on environmental citizenship. In a very real way, the book sets the table for an intense conversation yet to come. It is a start.

We must never forget that the author, in selecting the subtitle to this book, set out to describe an unnatural history of family and place. "Unnatural history" suggests that an element of the natural history had somehow become disordered. The environmental disaster went beyond the flooding; the environment itself had become carcinogenic. In portraying how environmental disorder played out in her own life experience, Williams succeeded in combining personal and natural history in a new way, modeling a literary form of natural history where memoir finally found its place. Ultimately, this presented the opportunity to link environmental health with human health through a family's lived experience.

Braiding Sweetgrass: Indigenous Wisdom, Scientific Knowledge, and the Teachings of Plants by Robin Wall Kimmerer (2013)

Action on behalf of life transforms. Because the relationship between self and the world is reciprocal, it is not a question of first getting enlightened or saved and then acting. As we work to heal the earth, the earth heals us. —FROM THE CHAPTER, "THE SACRED AND THE SUPERFUND"

In 1953, Professors James Watson and Francis Crick announced the discovery of the DNA molecule, the United States Congress passed a resolution advocating the termination of Native American tribal rights, and Joseph Stalin died. There were many firsts that year: Ian Fleming published *Casino Royale*, the first James Bond novel; Tenzing Norgay and Sir Edmund Hillary become the first mountaineers to ascend Mount Everest; and Hugh Hefner published the first issue of *Playboy Magazine*. In the midst of all this, Robin Wall Kimmerer was born in the open country of upstate New York.

Kimmerer is an enrolled member of the Citizen Potawatomi Nation. During her formational years, her parents were eager to reconnect with their Potawatomi heritage and encouraged Robin's familiarity with the natural environment. She spent a great deal of time outdoors as a child, collecting seeds and pressing leaves, storing these treasures in shoeboxes under her bed. Later, she trained as a botanist and plant ecologist, ultimately specializing in the ecology of mosses. A lifelong professor after earning her doctorate, she teaches at the State University of New York's College of Environmental Science and Forestry and is known for her work combining traditional ecological knowledge with environmental science.

One of the most telling snippets of memoir in *Sweetgrass* is where Kimmerer relates meeting with an advisor to enroll in classes when she first entered college. She told the advisor that she had chosen to study botany "because I wanted to learn about why asters and goldenrod looked so beautiful together." The advisor was not impressed, to Kimmerer's surprise, and responded, "I must tell you that that is not science. That is not at all the sort of thing with which botanists concern themselves." But he enrolled her in a general botany course so that she could learn what botany was really about. Kimmerer concludes this anecdote, "And so it began."

Despite her years within academe, much of Kimmerer's life has been a process of reconnection with traditional ecological knowledge. Her grandfather had been sent to a boarding school, the Carlisle Indian Industrial School, which was part of a systematic effort to eliminate Indigenous ways of speaking and thinking. Kimmerer describes the school's mission thus:

> Forced assimilation, the government policy to deal with the so-called Indian problem, shipped Mohawk children to the barracks at Carlisle, Pennsylvania, where the school's avowed mission was "Kill the Indian to Save the Man." Braids were cut off and Native languages forbidden. Girls were trained to cook and clean and wear white gloves on Sunday. The scent of sweetgrass was replaced by the soap smells of the barracks laundry. Boys learned sports and skills useful to a settled village life: carpentry, farming, and how to handle money in their pockets.

To appreciate *Sweetgrass*, one needs to understand that Kimmerer's lifelong mission as both a learner and an educator has been to create a dialogue between the science she learned as a plant ecologist with the traditional ecological knowledge she should have learned from tribal sources had it not been for programs of forced assimilation. She has, for example, undertaken to learn the Algonquian language of the Potawatomi, just as she had to learn the language of science. She writes, "We may not have wings or leaves, but we humans do have words. Language is our gift and our responsibility. I've come to think of writing as an act of reciprocity with the living land."

My electronic copy of *Braiding Sweetgrass* tells me that the word "language" appears 139 times in the book. A close reading of the first paragraph of the book's preface will illustrate not only how language becomes a motif in *Braiding Sweetgrass* but also what a joy it is to read prose so carefully crafted:

Hold out your hands and let me lay upon them a sheaf of freshly picked sweetgrass, loose and flowing, like newly washed hair. Golden green and glossy above, the stems are banded with purple and white where they meet the ground. Hold the bundle up to your nose. Find the fragrance of honeyed vanilla over the scent of river water and black earth and you understand its scientific name: *Hierochloe odorata*, meaning the fragrant, holy grass. In our language it is called *wiingaashk*, the sweet-smelling hair of Mother Earth. Breathe it in and you start to remember things you didn't know you'd forgotten.

Note that in the book's first sentence she addresses the reader directly using the second-person pronoun, "you." The author respects a response from the reader, something more than being entertained by the writing. She rewards the willingness to respond, even though it's symbolic at this point, with lush description that includes the feel, the color, and the smell of the plant specimen. She engages in metaphor here, "like newly washed hair," which signals that this is not scientific writing. Then, without having to point it out specifically, the writer highlights the correspondence between interpretations of the scientific name and its Indigenous counterpart. There is nothing in *Hierochloe odorata* that disputes *wiingaashk*. The final sentence, "Breathe it in and you start to remember things you didn't know you'd forgotten" portends the book's thesis, that plants can teach us things. Important things.

In the preface's second paragraph, she teaches us how to braid sweetgrass, a process that involves two people, a holder and a braider. And then, in the third paragraph, she asks, "Will you hold the end of the bundle while I braid?" This is how an elder teaches a child, how knowledge is passed along. There's no lecture here; it's all about participation, and the author promises that, once she's done braiding, she will hold the bundle for you while you braid.

There is one last paragraph in the preface, and it begins with an Indigenous concept of ownership. Kimmerer explains that she could hand us a braid of sweetgrass, but it's not hers to give, nor yours to take. "*Wiingaashk* belongs to herself." "So I offer, in its place," Kimmerer writes, "a braid of stories meant to heal our relationship with the world. This braid is woven from three strands: indigenous ways of knowing, scientific knowledge, and the story of an Anishinaabekwe scientist trying to bring them together in service to what matters most."

She has thrown the reader a curve here: *Anishinaabekwe*. From the capitalization, we can deduce that it's a proper noun, but beyond that most readers will not understand that the word is gendered, denoting a woman member of the Anishinaabe people. That the majority of her readers would not have understood this is okay, strangely. In Kimmerer's world view, taken from the last sentence of the prologue, "people and land are good medicine for each other." We will learn to appreciate language in this book, but we will also learn not to let language get in the way.

A phenomenon I've noted since the publication of *Braiding Sweetgrass* in 2013 is the number of students, especially environmental studies students, who have found the book transformative. A few, after discovering the book themselves, have emailed to ask whether I've read the book, one adding that if I haven't yet read it, I should put everything down and read it at once. It's worthwhile to investigate why the book has created such resonance with Millennials.

The book is divided into five sections: "Planting Sweetgrass," "Tending Sweetgrass," "Picking Sweetgrass," "Braiding Sweetgrass," and "Burning Sweetgrass." While this is a structure that should invigorate most readers, the author is careful not to oversimplify the process of learning. In the first chapter, "Skywoman Falling," after Kimmerer narrates the creation story of how Skywoman fell to the earth and endowed it with plants, she tells the story of teaching an early morning lecture class on Mondays, Wednesdays, and Fridays where she asked her general ecology students to list positive interactions between humans and the environment. She relates that the median response was "none." She reflects on this in the context of imagining a path forward toward ecological and cultural sustainability:

> I was stunned. How is it possible that in twenty years of education they cannot think of any beneficial relationships between people and the environment? Perhaps the negative examples they see every day—brownfields, factory farms, suburban sprawl—truncated their ability to see some good between humans and the earth. As the land becomes impoverished, so too does the scope of their vision. When we talked about this after class, I realized that they could not even imagine what beneficial relations between their species and others might look like.

There are two things happening here that I feel will stimulate readers who are contemporaries of Kimmerer's students. First, Kimmerer provides a mindset that investigates how not all human interaction with the environment is negative. We can and sometimes do have a positive environmental impact. Second, Kimmerer's approach to science is more dynamic than what they've previously experienced, one where traditional ecological knowledge contributes something to and learns something from a traditional scientific approach. In Kimmerer's worldview, the disjunction between an Indigenous approach and a scientific approach results from a false dichotomy. While modern Western culture may be one of discord and division, the natural world doesn't correspond to such partitioning. There is room within the ecosystem for multiple approaches.

Kimmerer contrasts the creation stories of Skywoman and Eve. In one story the woman is an ancestral gardener, helping to co-create "the good green world." In the other, the woman is an exile "just passing through an alien world on a rough road to her real home in heaven." It's especially fun when Kimmerer imagines a conversation between Eve and Skywoman, a chat in which the latter says, "Sister, you got the short end of the stick." This is perhaps where Millennials resonate with Kimmerer's cultural critique. In my experience as an educator, a great number of undergraduate students have already given up on the creation narrative of the Judeo-Christian scriptures because of how it commissions humanity to subdue and dominate. It's nice to consider an alternative mythology.

Kimmerer emerges early in the book as an accomplished storyteller. One of my favorite stories, in the chapter "The Council of Pecans," recalls her grandfather as a boy, wandering home barefoot in Oklahoma, stubbing a toe on a ripened pecan that had fallen into the grass. He and his brother stuff their pockets full, but there are still plenty of pecans to be collected, so the boys take off their trousers, knot the legs at the ankles, and stuff them full. She paints the scene of the boys running home after their Mama hollers for them, "their skinny legs pumping and their underpants flashing white in the fading light. It looks like they're each carrying a big forked log, hung like a yoke over their shoulders." She reflects that her grandpa would laugh to know that he was remembered not as a decorated World War I veteran but as a barefoot boy running home in his underpants. But she also reflects as an ecologist about the phenomenon of mast fruiting, which to her is a real-world parable about the power of unity. She concludes that reflection with the warrant: "All flourishing is mutual," which in its brevity is one of the best warrants in the book.

As a teacher of environmental writing and literature, I strove for many years to get my students to include warrants in their rhetorical arsenals as a way to support the claims they made. A warrant is a short wisdom utterance presented as a universal statement of fact, often at the end of a paragraph. Kimmerer's writing is a fine exemplar of the use of warrants. Included among my favorites from *Braiding Sweetgrass* are these:

- "The land knows you, even when you are lost."
- "What lies beyond our grasp remains unnamed."
- "To learn again, you really have to listen."
- "Plants tell their stories not by what they say, but by what they do."
- "Not everything should be convenient."
- "Sustain the ones who sustain you and the earth will last forever."
- "Language is the dwelling place of ideas that do not exist anywhere else."
- "Losing a plant can threaten a culture in much the same way as losing a language."
- "In a world of scarcity, interconnection and mutual aid become critical for survival."
- "The philosophy of reciprocity is beautiful in the abstract, but the practical is harder."
- "If a maple is an *it*, we can take up the chain saw. If a maple is a *her*, we think twice."

There is humor as well, interspersed among the warrants. Many of these relate to Kimmerer's work as a scientist, such as, "I've never met an ecologist who came to the field for a love of data or the wonder of a p-value." She makes herself the butt of much of this humor, especially in terms of teaching as a new PhD, and the process of having to reclaim "that other way of knowing that I had helplessly let science supplant." She never rejects her scientist side but writes about the tension between scientific method and her tendency to seek the threads that tend to join the world, noting that "science is rigorous in separating the observer from the observed, and the observed from the observer." Clearly that sort of separation was not going to work for Robin Wall Kimmerer. But there is a great deal of humility found in these reflections, especially when she observes, "As an enthusiastic young PhD, colonized by the arrogance of science, I had been fooling myself that I was the only teacher. The land is the real teacher."

If the land is the teacher in Kimmerer's world, trees are the master teachers. The word "tree" is mentioned 306 times in the book, with individual species sometimes capitalized, here noted in order of the number of their mentions: Maples, 130; Cedars, 86; Birches, 35; Black Ashes, 29; Pines, 17, Oaks, 12. Playing a lesser role in the agenda, Apples, Pecans, Witch Hazel and Basswoods are mentioned no more than seven times each. This is intriguing in that Kimmerer, a bryologist, only mentions moss 54 times. "Sweetgrass," interestingly enough is mentioned 131 times, only once more than maples. It might be worthwhile for the reader to investigate what's so special about maples that they could compete with *Hierochloe odorata* in a book about sweetgrass.

In the chapter "Maple Sugar Moon," we learn that the yard of Kimmerer's farmhouse in Fabius, New York, "is graced with seven Maples, big ones, planted almost two hundred years ago to shade the house." She adds that the largest tree "is as wide at its base as our picnic table is long." When they moved into the place, Kimmerer's daughters found the accoutrements of gathering maple sap in the loft above the stable. They scrubbed the mouse droppings out of the buckets and read up on the sugaring process while waiting for spring. Kimmerer notes that "Maples have a far more sophisticated system for detecting spring than we do," and then describes the light-absorbing pigments, phytochromes, that act as photosensors for the trees.

As is typical with Kimmerer's writing, the narrative bounces back and forth between science and metaphor. Within a few paragraphs, she describes the varied pitch of each bucket: "*Plink, ploink, plonk*—the tin buckets and their tented tops reverberate with every drop and the yard is singing. This is spring music as surely as the cardinal's insistent whistle." After that comes an extraordinary paragraph that Kimmerer writes less as a scientist or a storyteller and more as a mother:

> My girls watch in fascination. Each drop is as clear as water but somehow thicker, catching the light and hanging for a second at the end of the spile, growing invitingly into a larger and larger drop. The girls stretch out their tongues and slurp with a look of bliss, and unaccountably I am moved to tears. It reminds me of when I alone fed them. Now, on sturdy young legs, they are nursed by a maple—as close as they can come to being suckled by Mother Earth.

I found it interesting, when close reading the above paragraph, to observe that "maple" was not capitalized in this instance. Other times, when the writing turns mythopoeic, it is capitalized, as in the sentence, "The Maple is the leader of the trees, to recognize its gift of sugar when the People need it most." However, in a sentence that reflects traditional ecological values, it is not capitalized: "Our traditional thinking had it right: maples are people, people are maples." Kimmerer explains the grammar behind this in the notes at the end of the book, pointing out that we would never write about "george washington" without capitalizing those words so as not to strip him of his status as a human. To Kimmerer, this human exceptionalism is errant because it maintains that we are somehow different and indeed better than the other species who surround us. Therefore, she explains her breaking of such conventions thus: "So in this book as in my life, I break with those grammatical blinders to write freely of Maple, Heron, and Wally when I mean a person, human or not; and of maple, heron, and human when I mean a category or concept."

As a fellow writer who focuses on the more-than-human world, I find it instructive that Kimmerer waits until the end of the book to explain her grammar rather than using a more conventional, deductive approach to unveil her stylistic protocols in the introductory material, prior to when her punctuation becomes confusing. Writers are educators, especially those of us who write nonfiction, and Kimmerer the educator has made a decision that her readers should learn inductively, experiencing particular usage first and building toward the general concept in the end. This is probably more consistent with how children acquire traditional ecological knowledge within Indigenous communities. And Kimmerer probably doesn't mind that she may startle or even confuse those of us reading from the perspectives of Eurocentric grammar conventions. It's good for us to have our rattles shaken from time to time.

I note that the first sentence of the brief biography on Kimmerer's website, robinwallkimmerer.com, reads, "Robin Wall Kimmerer is a mother, scientist, decorated professor, and enrolled member of the Citizen Potawatomi Nation." This is intentional, that she lists her role as mother first, and she has said on many occasions that motherhood is her greatest role in life. One of the chapters I remember most from my first reading of *Braiding Sweetgrass*, "A Mother's Work," which goes to the process of finding and establishing the place into which she and her two daughters would make a home. The first objective toward this end was to cobble together tree forts in the two maples with low branches, one fort for each daughter. That task complete, Kimmerer wrote, "Being the good mother, good enough for two parents, seemed within my grasp. All that remained to complete the wish list for home was a swimmable pond."

The property had a spring-fed pond, one that in the past was a place where boys would park their wagons after haying and then skinny dip to clean up. But in recent times, Kimmerer relates, "It was so choked with green that you could not tell where weeds left off and water began." The pond was a victim of eutrophication, and Kimmerer realized that she would need to turn back time to return the pond to a swimmable ecosystem. At first she tried to skim off the algae but soon realized that this process was useless because she was dealing with the problem's symptom, not its cause. Then she tried shoveling the muck coating the pond's bottom but discovered that shoveling muck is "like trying to catch wind in a butterfly net." At that point she turned to science, writing: "A mat of algae is really nothing more than dissolved phosphorous and nitrogen made solid through the alchemy of photosynthesis." She created a plan to capture the nutrients in plants and haul those plants away before they could once again be turned into algae, but as a biologist she knew that first she'd have to identify what species of algae she was dealing with. She referred the problem to her microscope.

It took a year, ultimately, to win the battle, a year in which Kimmerer states that she developed a new relationship with mud. But she reflects on this critically, writing:

> Raking a pond provides you with a lot of mental free space for philosophizing. As I raked and plucked [tadpoles], it challenged my conviction that all lives are valuable, protozoan or not. As a theoretical matter, I hold this to be true, but on a practical level it gets murky, the spiritual and the pragmatic bumping heads. With every rake I knew that I was prioritizing. Short, single-cell lives were ended because I wanted a clear pond. I'm bigger, I have a rake, so I win. That's not a worldview I readily endorse.

Continuing on her quest, she discovered that when she cut the willows at the pond's edge they would grow back quickly, and by removing those branches she was removing nutrients from the pond. In the process, however, she realized that in creating the home she wanted for her children, she was "jeopardized the homemaking of other mothers whose intents were no different from mine." And she reflected further, "We set ourselves up as arbiters of what is good when often our standards of goodness are driven by narrow interests, by what we want." She continued to work on the pond, however, for years and years, ultimately realizing that she was creating a space in which her grandchildren would be able to play. This alleviated her philosophical quandaries somewhat, when she finally concluded, "A good mother grows into a richly eutrophic old woman, knowing that her work doesn't end until she creates a home where all of life's beings can flourish. There are grandchildren to nurture, and frog children, nestlings, goslings, seedlings, and spores, and I still want to be a good mother."

Kimmerer's honesty about the conflict between her deep values and noble motives, a clash that tended to create murky water, is a lesson in environmental writing. The path forward is not always clear, even for those schooled in both science and traditional ecological knowledge. For Kimmerer, writing as someone aspiring to be a good mother, the tiebreaker was to consider what was best for her grandchildren even though that decision still left her a bit conflicted. Compare this with other environmental writers for whom the path forward is crystal clear, never murky, and fundamentally judgmental, and we can see why Kimmerer has such a strong following among those who are new to environmental discourse. Her humility builds trust with her readers, just as her honesty demonstrates trust in them. The relationship is reciprocal.

There is a certain pathos in Kimmerer's writing that reinforces her authorial voice. In the first sentence of the next chapter, "The Consolation of Water Lilies," she writes, "Before I knew it, and long before the pond was ready for swimming, they were gone." Her daughters had moved away from home, both having packed off to college. She reflects that "it is the fundamental unfairness of parenthood that if we do our jobs well, the deepest bond we are given will walk out the door with a wave over the shoulder." Following the path blazed by Terry Tempest Williams, she is mixing personal history with natural history in the form of memoir, breaking with a longstanding genre norm to exclude family or other love interests from the text.* Kimmerer has made the decision not to hold the reader at arm's length with regard to her personal life; her experience of motherhood is integral to her experience of the more-than-human world. That connectedness between the human and nature, a connection where she views other animals as persons, is reflected directly in how Kimmerer structures her narrative.

Where Kimmerer's sense of nature differs from those whose work has been examined previously in this study is in how culture reinforces her connectedness with the biotic world. To Kimmerer, the dualism between nature and culture is unlocked because what she perceives as natural is also cultural. Her worldview flat-out refuses to distinguish between the wild and the civilized. Part of this is traditional, as when she writes: "Potawatomi stories remember that all the plants

---

* Off the top of my head I can think of very few nature writers writing before the 1990s who included family in their work, the most notable being Joseph Wood Krutch in his 1961 book, *The Forgotten Peninsula: A Naturalist in Baja, California*. Krutch had been accompanied by his wife, Marcelle, throughout most of his extensive travels through the Baja peninsula.

and animals, including humans, used to speak the same language. We could share with one another what our lives were like. But that gift is gone and we are the poorer for it." The greater part of it, however, is aspirational, such as in this sense: "Cultures of gratitude must also be cultures of reciprocity. Each person, human or no, is bound to every other in a reciprocal relationship. Just as all beings have a duty to me, I have a duty to them." In *Braiding Sweetgrass*, the traditional unfolds into the aspirational, and this is a major part of the book's rhetorical craft.

There were times, reading *Braiding Sweetgrass*, when I realized how deeply different Kimmerer's cultural experience of nature is than my own, and yet at other points in the narration I discover, to my delight, that we have shared many similar cultural experiences. I found this happening more than anywhere else in the chapter "Shkitagen: People of the Seventh Fire," where Kimmerer describes having learned to build a proper campfire from her father. When she writes, "He never said so directly, but fire making was more than just a woodcraft skill—to build a good fire, a person had to work," it sounds as if she's talking about my father rather than hers. Same when she tells the reader, "We earned high praise for the ideal one-match fire, but plenty of encouragement if we needed a dozen." And yet there are differences, such as when she confides, "I found a secret that always worked for me: to sing to the fire as I touched the match to tinder." I would love to hear her song.

One doesn't have to agree with Kimmerer to benefit from how she understands nature. When she claims that the arrogance of English is that the only way to be animate is to be human, I can cite numerous exceptions where the grammar of animacy is present, especially in English-language nature poetry. Despite those exceptions, however, it's important to understand the perspective from whence her claim originates. This could be helpful for those engaged in wildlife conservation and habitat restoration, where difficult decisions, such as culling trees to restore wetlands, must be made. We should ask how such decisions can be arrived at in the most respectful way no matter how disquieting it might be to do so. Any conservationist who doesn't respect a tree really doesn't understand trees.

The final full chapter of the book, "Defeating Windigo," adheres to a grammar entirely its own where the first page is all in italic font. There she uses the first-person present tense to narrate a poignant event: *"In the spring I walk across the meadow toward my medicine woods, where the plants give their gifts with unstinting generosity. It is mine not by deed, but by care. I've come here for decades to be with them, to listen, to learn, and to gather."* She feels a chill as she walks, and then notices the deep ruts of logging trucks. While the spring flowers she seeks are still there, the trees no longer are. She explains that her neighbor brought in the loggers over the winter, and then writes, "There are so many ways to harvest honorably, but he chose otherwise."

At the end of the italicized section, Kimmerer laments, "*I fear that a world made of gifts cannot coexist with a world made of commodities. I fear that I have no power to protect what I love against the Windigo.*"

Kimmerer makes no effort to describe the Windigo of Algonquian legend except contextually in one sentence where she refers to it as a monster. We get no sense of this monster's appearance, which perhaps makes it easier for us to deduce that the Windigo is capitalism itself, "the unholy coupling of greed and growth and carbon" that produces "economies that are based on constant taking without giving in return." If not capitalism, then at least materialism.

Kimmerer notes that the Windigo is more powerful in the winter, in times of scarcity, and that in legends it could be defeated by heroic action during the summer, a time of plenty. She opines that we need more than just a change of our economic systems to defeat Windigo, we ultimately need a change of heart. "Scarcity and plenty are as much qualities of the mind and spirit as they are of the economy. Gratitude plants the seed for abundance."

What she wrote next blows my mind: "Each of us comes from people who were once indigenous. We can reclaim our membership in the cultures of gratitude that formed our old relationships with the living earth. Gratitude is a powerful antidote to Windigo psychosis. A deep awareness of the gifts of the earth and of each other is medicine."

The final pages of the chapter switch back to an italic font and narrate Kimmerer's personal battle with Windigo. It's a good story, especially the ending, where the heroine sits down beside the vanquished monster and says, "Let me tell you a story."

—————

The day I began the rough draft of this chapter, Kimmerer was awarded a MacArthur Fellowship, the so-called "genius grant," along with the final author featured in this study, J. Drew Lanham. From the perspective of expanding the culture of literary natural history, I can't imagine two more worthy recipients. Congratulations to them both.

The Home Place: Memoirs of a Colored Man's Love Affair with Nature by J. Drew Lanham (2016)

I've watched hawks trace circles in the sky, connecting one circuit to another. I imagine they start these journeys by looking up. —FROM THE CHAPTER, "LITTLE BROWN ICARUS"

Early in 1965, Malcom X was assassinated by three men in Manhattan while preparing to address the Organization of Afro-American Unity, a group that he had founded. His autopsy revealed twenty-one gunshot wounds to his body. A month later, Martin Luther King Jr. led a five-day, fifty-four-mile march from Selma, Alabama, to the state capitol in Montgomery in a nonviolent show of support for voting rights. This was one of three Selma marches organized that year, one of which resulted in the "Bloody Sunday" incident where dozens of demonstrators were hospitalized after being beaten by police while crossing the Selma bridge. Images of the violence were broadcast on national television, horrifying viewers and engendering support for the civil rights movement. That same year the Voting Rights Act became law.

The Autobiography of Malcom X, coauthored with Alex Hailey, was published in October of 1965, nine months after the assassination. *The Sound of Music, Dr. Zhivago,* and *Thunderball,* respectively, were the three top-grossing movies that year. Other notable 1965 milestones included the completion of the Gateway Arch in St. Louis, Missouri, the conclusion of the Gemini manned space program, the creation of the Medicare program by President Lyndon Johnson as part of his

"War on Poverty," and the birth of J. Drew Lanham in a segregated hospital in Augusta, Georgia.

The Home Place: Memoirs of a Colored Man's Love Affair with Nature follows the classical form of a memoir, tracking the author's ancestry and parentage, childhood, coming of age, academic achievement and professional development, all with an emphasis on cultural history. It differs from the other books included in this volume in that it views natural history primarily through the lens of memory, for the most part eschewing contemporaneous observations of the natural world. This approach is compelling because such a large part of Lanham's audience will never have perused the reflections of an African American naturalist/ornithologist. There is a novel tale here begging to be told, not in the language of social theory, but in the form of a renewed Black narrative. Lanham alludes to this at the end of the book's introduction, where he states, "I believe the best way to begin reconnecting humanity's heart, mind, and soul to nature is for us to share our individual stories. This is my contribution to that greater mission; sometimes the words that make the fragmented more whole need to come from someone in a different skin."

Lanham grew up in Edgefield, in rural South Carolina, where as a boy he was particularly attuned to the natural world. He writes:

> I craved knowledge about the wildlife that lived around us. I read every book I could about the creatures that shared the Home Place kingdom with me. I pored over encyclopedias and piled up library fines. Field guides were treasure troves of information: pictures stacked side by side with brief descriptions of what, where, and when. I went back outdoors, where I walked, stalked, and waited to see as many wild things as I could. I collected tadpoles to watch them grow into froglets; I caught butterflies and gazed into their thousand-lensed eyes. Birds were everywhere and as I learned to identify them by sight their songs sunk into my psyche, too. Nature was often the first and last thing on my mind, morning to night.

Lanham's family lived on a farm adjacent to a homestead where his grandparents lived. When his grandfather died, Lanham took up residency with his grandmother in order to keep her company and help out around the house. She had been born in 1896, "one generation removed from slavery." Although staunchly Christian, she was also deeply superstitious, and Lanham confesses that, when he finally moved "into the modern world" to attend college, he still believed many of the superstitions he'd been taught.

Lanham's father was born in 1928, the year Herbert Hoover was elected president. As a consequence, the name "Hoover" had been bestowed on the senior Lanham. The junior Lanham writes that he and his father were especially close: "To me Hoover was everyman: teacher, coach, mechanic, plumber, cattleman, farmer, lumberjack, husband, brother, son, and father. He had to be all those things because his family's survival depended on the plowing, cutting, feeding, loading, and fixing that made things go and grow." Hoover taught his son essential woodcraft and field etiquette as well as hunting and fishing skills. Lanham notes that "Home Place," as they knew their farm, was not a democracy. Lanham was taught to respect and obey all adults, and if there was any failure to adhere to the three basic rules of respect, obedience, or performance, there would be a "whippin'" often administered with a switch or a leather belt. Lanham observes that while he loved his parents, "I've long found it ironic that any black people, coming through the civil rights movement, witnessing all the violence the period brought to bear, and with their parents born at the edge of slavery, would carry the whip forward as a means of control. I've tried to do better with my own children."

Although I am Lanham's senior by more than a decade, if I had read the first half of his memoir stripped of dates and historical references, I would have thought myself younger than him. Much of this is cultural, how his experience growing up as a rural Black southerner contrasts with my experience growing up as a suburban White Coloradan. This disjunction extends to all elements of cultural experience, from family routine to economics to education and especially to religious adherence. As a reader from outside Lanham's ethnic, regional culture, it was sometimes challenging for me to understand how much of this was due to the contrasts between the Deep South and the Mountain or Coastal West, and how much was because of race. I suppose it might have been equal parts of each: for example, at one point in the chapter "First-Sunday God," he writes, poignantly, "Black folks and church in the South are stuck fast together like the cockleburs on a dog's back."

Although Lanham and I shared such experiences as doctoral studies and teaching at the university level, I was especially troubled by the divergence of our experience in academe. I can't remember a single instance during my ten years of postgraduate studies where I felt fearful for my safety. For Lanham, this was a common experience, especially during field research. For example, in the chapter "Birding While Black," he writes of an experience where he felt it unsafe to conduct his doctoral research: "In remote places fear has always accompanied binoculars, scopes, and field guides as baggage. A few years later, during my doctoral field research, three raggedy, red spray-painted Ks appeared on a Forest Service gate leading to one of my study sites. When I saw the "welcome" sign, many of the old feelings came back. I instinctively looked over my shoulder to see if anyone was watching. And I didn't visit the point again. My safety compromised, I found another place to do the science."

When reading this passage the first time, I realized that during my years in the classroom I'd often assigned field projects to students and research assistants without concerning myself for a moment about their feelings of safety. Perhaps this was my own naïveté, but such considerations were never part of my student, teaching, or supervision experiences. I regret this in hindsight, and I can only hope that none of the students of color with whom I was associated ever felt fear for their physical safety as the result of having been assigned field work.

For Lanham, the incident with the KKK graffiti was not an isolated one, and many were equally egregious. He wrote, for example, of a time when he had proposed a project for potentially ground-breaking research in the Southern Appalachians regarding rose-breasted grosbeaks and golden-winged warblers, a project for which he'd already applied for funding, that had to be abandoned because it was near a place where white supremacists gathered for target practice shooting at silhouettes of Martin Luther King Jr. Before abandoning his project, someone at his university joked that his degree might have to be awarded posthumously.

Having chosen a career in wildlife biology, Lanham realized that his profession would require him to conduct research in remote places, and that his credibility "would be shattered if I showed hesitation in venturing out beyond some negro-safe zone of comfort." He had to make a conscious decision to swallow his fear and move on. Is it any wonder that fields such as wildlife biology are less diverse than they ought to be? It's one thing to worry about sharks and bears, but something altogether worse to have to fret about appearing in the gunsights of white supremacists.

Lanham's "Birding While Black" concept has had resonance beyond the thus-named chapter from *Home Place*. Before the book was published, an excerpt was released in *Literary Hub*, the first sentence grabbing the world's attention: "It's only 9:06 A.M., and I think I might get hanged today." Lanham has also lectured on this topic as a visitor to other universities and has participated in a "Birding While Black" podcast with the American Birding Association, a conversation where birding is described as "the whitest thing you can do."

I had been exposed to Lanham's "Birding While Black" theme via two short articles published in *Orion Magazine*, "9 Rules for Black Birdwatchers" (October

23, 2013), and "9 Rules for the Woke Birdwatcher" (December 3, 2020).* These pieces are laced with irony and wit and demonstrate a different facet of Lanham's prose than are found in the memoir, where the author's voice takes on more of a narrative aspect, resonating with thoughtfulness and reverence.

While Lanham goes to considerable length in *Home Place* to avoiding politicizing his experience, he is critical of his hometown's lack of equity and diversity despite it being "a rich refuge for wild things." In what is perhaps the harshest such critique in the book, he writes, "Edgefield has been less welcoming of—and less of a refuge for—human diversity. Under regressive and racist governors who fostered exclusion and violence, the power base in Edgefield kept things stuck in a state of antebellum stagnation, separate and nowhere near equal."

Aldo Leopold is mentioned fifteen times in *Home Place*. Lanham writes, "When I read *A Sand County Almanac*, Aldo Leopold, a dead white man I'd never heard of, from someplace I'd never been, suddenly became an inspirational mentor." This mentorship led not only to his writing career but also toward studying wildlife biology and ultimately becoming a professor of that subject, following the lead of America's first-ever professor of wildlife biology. Lanham appreciates Leopold's philosophical approach to writing, his lyricism, and the fact that Leopold saw love as being central to his land ethic. Lanham writes, unreservedly, "The ideas captured me. His writings were poetry more than prose, and they danced in my imagination. I was in love. The book would become sacred to me. It was my catalyst."

We should investigate Lanham's declaration that Leopold's essays were more poetry than prose. Behind this plaudit lies the fact that Lanham is a poet himself. Although his poetry is of lesser renown than his prose, it is an important part of his oeuvre, as is demonstrated by his second book, *Sparrow Envy: A Field Guide to Birds and Lesser Beasts,* published five years after *Home Place* came out. Selections from the collection have been republished in several anthologies, and the work exhibits more of Lanham's comic wit than his memoir. The final poem in the collection, "Group Think: New Names for Plural Birds" is one of my favorite Lanham poems. In it, he proposes new collective nouns for bird species, including "Privilege" for any flock of white birds, "though it's not their fault / for almost always being given the benefit of the doubt / or being / mostly respected; usually liked."

---

* The articles are currently available to read on *Orion*'s website. "9 Rules for Black Birdwatchers" was also reprinted in Lanham's 2021 poetry collection, *Sparrow Envy.*

Following his poetic leanings, Lanham's word usage throughout the memoir is strongly individualistic, perhaps even stubbornly so. The most notable among these usages for me is the word "colored" in the title. When I was a boy, this adjective was generally considered the polite way to reference a person of African American heritage, but that usage soon fell out of favor, perhaps because it was used graphically during segregation times to indicate the drinking fountains and restrooms that Black citizens were permitted to use. While it has come back partially via the phrase "persons of color," Lanham not only reclaims the original version as a reference to himself, but redefines it in the process, writing, "My plumage is a kaleidoscopic rainbow of an eternal hope and the deepest blue of despair and darkness. All of these hues are me; I am, in the deepest sense, colored."

A close reading of the following paragraph will not only reveal Lanham's unsettled nature of being a Black birder, but also his careful use of language, especially where he employs ornithological jargon (underlined here for emphasis):

> Over the years I've <u>listed</u> hundreds of species in hundreds of places, from coast to coast and abroad, too. I've seen a <u>shit-ton</u> of birds from sea level to alpine tundra. But as a black·man in America I've grown up with a <u>profile</u>.* Society at large has certain boxes I'm supposed to fit into, and most of the labels on those boxes aren't good. Birders have a profile as well, a much more positively perceived one. Being a birder in the United States means that you're probably a middle-aged, middle-class, well-educated white man. While most of the labels apply to me, I am a black man and therefore <u>a birding anomaly</u>. The chances of seeing someone who looks like me while on the trail are only slightly greater than those of sighting <u>an ivory-billed woodpecker</u>. In my lifetime I've encountered fewer than ten black birders. We're true <u>rarities</u> in our own right.

Lanham begins this paragraph by establishing his bona fides as a birder, and the terminology he employs is purposeful. He has "listed" hundreds of birds, not

---

* Beginning a sentence with the conjunction "But" is a strong element of Lanham's rhetoric, occurring 127 times in the book. While old-school guides to word usage such as *Strunk and White's Elements of Style* may frown on such usage, most modern grammarians see nothing wrong with it. In Lanham's grammar, the sentence beginning with "But" tends to point out contrasts between how systems work within the privileged world of whiteness, but not in the world he experiences.

just observed them or identified them. All serious birders will recognize this verb, the past tense of "to list," implying that he maintains a life list, and we are left to understand that his list is impressive, both in terms of the scope of birds he has listed and their quantity. The adjective "shit-ton" tends to establish that he's not just an academic birder, not just an ornithologist who talks professor-speak, but an everyman sort of birder. But, Lanham tells us, he is a Black man and therefore has a profile. The word "profile" challenges the reader not to profile him, not only to circumvent microaggression, I would assume, but also to avoid boxing him in. Since Lanham's profile fits the stereotypical birder profile in all ways except one—he is not a white man—he self-identifies as "a birding anomaly." It's interesting to note that within ornithology, the term "anomaly" often references plumage of an unusual color, such as in leucistic plumage where some feathers lack pigment. The next sentence contains a reference that requires a bit of avian literacy to comprehend, when Lanham claims that the chances of seeing a Black man on the trail are only slightly greater than spotting an ivory-billed woodpecker, a bird thought by many to be extinct, but whose status continues to be controversial. If it is still extant, it can only be found in the most remote, inaccessible swamps of the Deep South. Now comes the concluding fact that in all his birding he has encountered fewer that ten Black birders. This leads him to claim to be a true rarity in the paragraph's final sentence. Birders will understand "rarity" to be a technical term denoting a species that is found outside of its normal range. Thus, he uses birding lingo to deconstruct his own standing within the birding community.

Lanham's many profiles throughout the book combine, on the surface level, to make him an enigma: birder, poet, hunter, educator, scientist, colored man, land owner, doctor of philosophy, believer in miracles, conservationist, professor, Southerner. Lanham seems to understand that people have a hard time pinning him down to type and at times seems to revel in this, such as in the passage: "A warbler migrated over hundreds of miles of land and ocean to sing in the same tree once again is as miraculous to be as any dividing sea. There is righteousness in conserving things, staving off extinction, and simply admiring the song of a bird. In my moments of confession in front of strangers, talking about my love of something much greater than any one of us, I become a freer me. Each time I am reborn."

The overall memoir is organized into three major sections: "Flock," which deals mostly with familial history; "Fledgling," which deals with Lanham's childhood growing up to the point when he was ready to disperse from his flock; and "Flight," which deals with Lanham's life after he left the family home. Clever as the ornithological Flock → Fledgling → Flight structure is, it could lead to the misleading impression that the book is wholly about its author's personal history. While this may be true on the surface level—the book is, after all, a memoir—I would make the case that the major theme throughout this book is how the environment has agency within the author's life. In essence, the environment is more than just a setting in which the narrative is framed. Rather, it's a dynamic presence that effects change.

I doubt that Lanham would disagree with my assessment here. He asserts as much in the second chapter of "The Flock," where he writes, "That is who we are as a species: not just aspirational but at a unique edge between evolution and technology. We adapt, we master; we are part of nature, we overcome it; we are shaped by history, we make it. And any one of our stories can thus be told twice, looking at the forces outside us and those within." The force outside us, as Lanham tells it, is nature. It is a dynamic force, portrayed as being always on the move where everything is either accelerating or slowing down. It is not merely physical reality, but spiritual as well. According to Lanham, "I've expanded the walls of my spiritual existence beyond the pews and pulpit to include longleaf savannas, salt marshes, cove forests, and tall-grass prairie. The miracles for me are in migratory journeys and moonlit nights. Swan song is sacred. Nature seems worthy of worship."

As the memoir develops, so does our understanding of the role the natural world plays in Lanham's life. In "The Flock," nature is Lanham's childhood fascination, whether it's collecting specimens, learning the names of animal species, or discovering "in every natural nook and cranny—a stump hole, a dry creek bed, or a burrow in the ground—there was something furred, feathered, finned, or scaled that scurried, swam, or flew. I was amazed by it all."

Early on in "The Fledgling," Lanham buys his first field guide and discovers the enormous number of birds he doesn't yet know and makes a conscious decision to pursue this knowledge. At this same time, he is learning life skills, everything from learning how to hunt with his first BB gun to learning how to tend farm animals. He is also learning important lessons about the nature of death, especially in terms of how his father's death led to the demise of the spring that provided the farm with life-giving water. Through this all, Lanham was learning to think critically about the natural world, a process that would provide direction for both his formal education and his career. Critically, at this point, it is nature doing the teaching.

In "The Flight," Lanham describes his early adult life as jumping through a series of hoops. Upon earning his bachelor's degree, he immediately considered postgraduate education, pausing only long enough to get married the day after commencement. Fatherhood followed quickly, another force of nature, and, after a few jobs doing field work in the great outdoors, he went back to school in pursuit of a PhD. Earning a doctorate surprised him—this was not as easy a hoop to jump through as he had anticipated. He confesses that he struggled mightily for the next five years: "My bird research project in the nearby Blue Ridge Mountains turned into a thick thorny tangle, constantly revealing new layers of complexity and logistical constraint that statistics didn't really want to solve. Days afield, armed with binoculars and data sheets, became wearisome." He persevered, however, landing a tenure-track appointment as his university and began jumping through a new set of hoops: gathering grants, publishing papers, teaching, and advising graduate students. Regardless, there were struggles: "Early on, a few fellow faculty members told me that I'd never make it—that my hire had been strictly an affirmative action move and progression through the ranks would be all but impossible."

They were wrong, of course. Dr. Lanham went on to become an endowed professor, a distinguished professor, a master teacher, and, a few years after *Home Place* was published, a MacArthur Fellow, this prestigious award noting his work "combining conservation science with personal, historical, and cultural narratives of nature."

Regardless of Lanham's career success as a scientist, there are several places within the book where he reflects on of the limitations of science. In the introduction, for example, he complains that science's tendency to make the miraculous mundane "is like replacing the richest artistry with paint-by-number portraits." He also worries about losing touch within the process of "grinding data through complex statistical packages." He wants to view conservation and even wildlife management as equal parts art and science and marvels at how this was accomplished within the management of his mother's homestead. In a few places, he gives the impression that these concerns are the result of his own maturing as a scientist, especially via statements such as this: "Within the past couple of years I've given fewer and fewer 'p-value' presentations. More and more I find myself taking the hard data and wrapping it in genuine caring. The science is critical; it is the 'scripture.' It always comes first. But action has to come behind it."

While racism is a constant backdrop for the book, it would miss the mark to presume that the book is about racism. Rather, it is about solutions, all of which filter through Lanham's understanding of nature. He claims nature as a place for all of humanity and suggests that the more we can get persons of color "out there," birding, hunting, hiking, and even training as wildlife biologists, the more we will discover the commonality of our species. He truly believes that "there is power in the shared pursuit of feathered things." This is not to say that he doesn't share painful memories, especially regarding childhood. One such recollection that I found to be particularly poignant was a grade-school memory of class picture day when brittle plastic combs were handed out, implements that were not intended to groom "tightly packed black-boy hair." Lanham writes, "When one of the combs broke off in my little Afro, classmates laughed. Afterward, I asked to wear my hair cut short so that grooming wasn't an issue."

Problem solved. Lanham continues to wear his hair short to this day, crew-cut short.

I find the structure of problem/solution to be one of the most compelling elements of this memoir. One can see how this resiliency has not only led to attaining his various life goals but also to crafting his understanding of his role in the world of conservation. A significant move here was to switch interests between the zoology he'd studied at the undergraduate and master's level to forestry and wildlife management for his doctoral studies. As he so eloquently put it, "My transition from a wine-drinking, cheese-eating ecologist to a beer-swilling, venison-chewing wildlife biologist came in my late twenties, as I moved closer to becoming Dr. Lanham." But this transition renewed his energy for his studies, and made him feel that he would be able to contribute more on a practical level, especially as someone who had grown up as a hunter. It was a solution that helped him reconcile academic and personal culture, all the while deepening his relationship with nature.

There is a grand hunting story included in the memoir about a jawbone that hangs on Lanham's office wall. It came from a large buck deer that he killed on his mother's 128-acre familial plot. Lanham had been hunting from a tree stand, his usual method, and wasn't able to get in a clean shot as the buck moved through. "The last I glimpsed of the biggest deer I'd ever seen was a white rear disappearing as fast as the front had come into view." The story goes on for pages—and I'd hate to spoil Lanham's hunting story for those who haven't yet read *Home Place*—but it's a story of respect, which is reflected by the hunter's actions at the conclusion of the hunt: "I knelt and felt the muscled power beneath the thick gray-brown coat, and the warmth of life cooling quickly away. I touched the stone-smooth coldness of the broad, cedar-stained antlers. I prayed to something for the luck and thanked the buck for his existence, given now to mine."

An academic myself, the chapter that had the greatest meaning for me is "A New Religion" that narrates a life-changing field trip Lanham took with students. At the beginning of the chapter, he explains that lecturing had always come easily to him, "but after many years of stale introductions, methods, results, and conclusions, I began to wonder if anyone was listening—and if there was real reason for them to." And then he took a group of graduate students to Warren Wilson, a small liberal-arts college in the mountains of western North Carolina, to hear E. O. Wilson speak.

Wilson, a Harvard biologist specializing in myrmecology, the study of ants, was a staggering intellect and is often referred to as the "father of sociobiology." He also co-authored the ecological theory of island biogeography, as well as being a best-selling writer with two Pulitzer Prizes to his credit. Lanham tells his readers that Wilson introduced the concepts of biodiversity and biophilia to the world and renders the high praise that "he's on par with Aldo Leopold and Rachel Carson."

Lanham's group gathered in the college chapel, finding space to sit on the floor. He tells us that, when Wilson mounted the pulpit and began to speak, he spoke softly of the need to notice nature. Lanham continued:

> There weren't any statistics, graphs, or scatterplots. There were no slides or pictures of devastated forests and animals dying in traps. His voice, even amplified through a microphone, never rose above the quiet surge of low-tide surf. Yet he was irresistibly compelling, magnetic. I was entranced. I looked around—everyone else was drawn in, too. There were nods of approval, and more than a few eyes glistened with tears. It was church like I'd never imagined it. There was no damnation or guilt, but simply a heart-filled plea to notice, nurture, and care.

Lanham reports that the evening planted a seed in him regarding "what might be in me." As a result of that, he spent time in northern Vermont, writing and reflecting about nature in different ways, and he became aware of his dissatisfaction with how he was pursuing academic advancement. It was a time of renewal that inspired change in many ways, even in simple terms. Lanham reports that "I shake hands less now and give hugs more. I exchange more heartbeats than business cards." There was a spiritual release as well where he "settled into a comfortable place with the idea of nature and god being the same thing." Among environmentalists, even among university professors, there are few who are able to go about their work with such a deep sense of mission.

In a chapter near the end of the book reflecting on the concept of land, appropriately titled "Thinking," Lanham states that "place and land and nature: how we tie these things together is critical to our sense of self-purpose and our fit in the world." While he thinks this is true of people everywhere, he feels that "nowhere is it truer than in the South." Lanham's concept of land has a lot to do with ownership. He wonders how other Black and Brown people think about land, including "how our lives would change for the better if the ties to place weren't broken by bad memories, misinformation, and ignorance." Previously, he had claimed that the scars of slavery were too fresh for many Black people, noting that "fields of cotton stretching to the horizon—land worked, sweated, and suffered over for the profit of others—probably don't engender warm feelings among most black people."

The very last reflection in the book, in a chapter called "Patchwork Legacy," focuses on a plot of land to which Lanham has family ties and which he affectionately refers to as "more than 120 acres of piedmont slate-belt woodland just begging for love and attention." Still under the influence of Aldo Leopold, he ruses about making that plot "a working refuge where wild things were the priority and where artful management might make a positive difference." Far removed from the Home Place where he grew up, he confesses that he's had to learn to love the other place because "it has another feel." He's not exactly sure why the feel is different and speculates that perhaps it's how the land lies on different rock, which makes it want to be part of the piedmont prairie. Regardless of the numerous other possibilities he lists as to why he might feel different about a place he's had to put in effort to learn to love, there is no question that what interests him most about the place is "a chance at reviving legacy."

Let's hope there's a Greenwood County almanac coming out soon about that revival.

Writing Nature: Convergences

Heaven is under our feet as well as over our heads. —THOREAU, *WALDEN*, FROM THE CHAPTER "THE POND IN WINTER"

While the nature writers comprising this study are a diverse group, there are definite convergences in outlook once we get past the propensity of these authors to march to different drummers. Obviously, they all savored their time in nature, be it the woods, the desert, the sea, a farm pasture, prairie, wetland, or creek. Less obvious is how hard they all worked at being attentive.

For many, the best way to achieve a satisfactory level of attentiveness was to spend time alone, beyond the distractions of society. For most, their process of attentiveness involved keeping a journal, or at least rigorous field notes. For all, their writing was intricately connected to the act of seeing. We could fill a volume with what Thoreau, Austin, Burroughs, Leopold, Carson, Abbey, Williams, Kimmerer, and Lanham have written about seeing, starting with Thoreau's dictum, "It's not what you look at that matters, it's what you see."

There is a sense of ecological wonder running through the works studied herein. I would theorize that the sublime is more readily apparent to those who are mindful about how they pay attention to the natural world. Simply put, as Mary Oliver pointed out in her prose poem, "Upstream:" *Attention is the beginning of devotion.*

Despite their reverence for nature, for the most part, our authors eschewed organized religion, at least in their maturity, and many wondered down the same road as John Burroughs into some form of pantheism. Or, as Lanham expressed it in his chapter, "New Religion," "I've settled into a comfortable place with the idea of nature and god being the same thing."

There is a didactic strain running through the works studied here. Each author wanted to teach the reader some fine point of natural history, especially one that would lead to greater appreciation of the natural world. Interestingly, the most didactic of our authors was Rachel Carson, the only author studied herein who was never employed as a teacher. Thoreau, Austin, and Burroughs each found teaching to be unsatisfying in the early years of their careers, but they all lectured successfully once they'd published books. Leopold, Abbey, Dillard, Williams, Kimmerer, and Lanham have taught extensively at the university level.

Lastly, they were all writers to the core. By this, I mean that they tended not to write just to make a living but that writing was a way of living a fuller life. Just as they interpreted nature through their writing, the writing completed the process of observing natural history. With that in mind, I will give the ten authors the final word on writing nature:

Henry David Thoreau, from his journal of September 1859: "A writer, a man writing, is the scribe of all nature; he is the corn and the grass and the atmosphere writing. It is always essential that we love to do what we are doing, do it with a heart. The maturity of the mind, however, may perchance consist with a certain dryness."

Mary Hunter Austin, from the Preface to *The Land of Little Rain*: "The earth is no wanton to give up all her best to every comer, but keeps a sweet, separate intimacy for each. But if you do not find it all as I write, think me not less dependable nor yourself less clever."

John Burroughs, from his journal of November 1884: "The greatest writer serves life, serves truth and art; art follows him and gathers up and makes much of what he drops."

Aldo Leopold, from the "December" chapter of *A Sand County Almanac*: "Books on nature seldom mention wind; they are written behind stoves."

Rachel Carson, from an unpublished paper, quoted in *The House of Life: Rachel Carson at Work* by Paul Brooks: "No writer can stand still. He continues to create or he perishes. Each task completed carries its own obligation to go on to something new."

Edward Abbey, from his book, *A Voice Crying in the Wilderness*: "Some people write to please, to soothe, to console. Others to provoke, to challenge, to exasperate and infuriate. I've always found the second approach the more pleasing."

Annie Dillard, from her book, *The Writing Life*: "I do not so much write a book as sit up with it, as a dying friend. I hold its hand and hope it will get better."

Terry Tempest Williams, from the prose poem "Why I Write," in *Red: Passion and Patience in the Desert*: "I write because it is dangerous, a bloody risk, like love, to form the words, to say the words, to touch the source, to be touched, to reveal how vulnerable we are, how transient. I write as though I am whispering in the ear of the one I love."

Robin Wall Kimmerer, from *Braiding Sweetgrass*: "For me, writing is an act of reciprocity with the world; it is what I can give back in return for everything that has been given to me. And now there's another layer of responsibility, writing on a thin sheet of tree and hoping the words are worth it. Such a thought could make a person set down her pen."

J. Drew Lanham, from his website: "I write to translate what my heart sees. I craft essays centered on place and a passion for wildness. I feel poetry and try to capture moments in words. . . . Coloring the conservation conversation is my mission. Words are my paint."

Acknowledgments

Much of my writing takes place in an eight-by-ten-foot outbuilding, the walls of which are constructed of trees I felled when we first moved to the San Juan Islands. In common parlance, it is called "The Writing Shack." The day after I completed a previous book project, after spending the morning attending to literary correspondence, I trudged back up to our cabin for lunch and reported that I didn't have another writing project lined up. Without hesitation, the woman to whom I dedicate all my books, who at that point had not yet retired, pointed a spousal index finger upward and said, "You're writing another book."

I asked what the book ought to be about, and she assured me that if I returned to the shack after lunch something worthwhile would come to me. I am grateful, as always, for her unwavering confidence and support, and I hope that this book qualifies as "something worthwhile."

I am grateful to a former dean of Santa Clara University's College of Arts and Sciences, Atom Yee, who treated me to lunch one day at the faculty club and suggested that perhaps the time had come for me to venture beyond academic writing and to consider writing as a public intellectual, his term, by which he meant to suggest that I should consider writing for a general audience. That luncheon was life-changing and, at this point, has resulted in the publication of three books, with at least one more to come.

I have reminisced often, throughout my time researching this study, about conversations with students in such courses as Nature and Imagination, Analyzing Green Rhetoric, Environmental Writing, Environmental Thought, Writing Natural History, Writing for the Birds, and Writing Nature. Over the years, I've gained valuable perspectives from my students regarding the works critiqued in this study, not only via our discussions but also by reading your papers. Thank you for your many insights.

I have long felt myself to be part of an extended community of writers concerned about the natural world and enamored of natural history. I am appreciative of all my naturalist colleagues and nature-writing mentors, especially two who illuminated my graduate studies, Sharman Apt Russel at Antioch University and Kathleen Jamie at the University of Stirling, both of whom are recipients of the John Burroughs Medal. Thanks also to Stanford University's Charlie Junkerman, who advised my thesis analyzing the rhetoric of Edward Abbey's *Desert Solitaire*.

I am grateful to the team at Michigan State University Press: Editorial Director Elizabeth Sherburn Demers, Managing Editor Kristine M. Blakeslee, Project Editor Amanda Frost, Editorial Assistant Liz Deegan, Marketing and Sales Manager Nicole Utter; and student assistant Megan Howarth. I'm grateful, as well, to the anonymous reviewers for sharing their considerable expertise in nature writing, for their generous critique, and for the time they invested in this book.

Works Cited

Abbey, Edward. *Desert Solitaire: A Season in the Wilderness*. New York: McGraw-Hill, 1968.

———. *The Journey Home: Some Words in Defense of the American West*. New York: Dutton, 1977.

———. *A Voice Crying in the Wilderness (Vox Clamantis in Deserto): Notes from a Secret Journal*. New York: St. Martin's Griffin, 1989.

Austin, Mary Hunter. *Earth Horizon*. Boston: Houghton Mifflin, 1932.

———. *Land of Little Rain*. Boston: Houghton Mifflin, 1903.

———. "Woman Alone." *Beyond Borders: The Selected Essays of Mary Austin*. Carbondale: Southern Illinois University Press, 1996.

Beebe, William. *The Book of Naturalists: An Anthology of the Best Natural History*. New York: Knopf, 1945.

Bergon, Frank. *A Sharp Outlook: Selected Natural History Essays of John Burroughs*. Washington, DC: Smithsonian Institution Press, 1987.

Berry, Thomas. *The Great Work: Our Way into the Future*. New York: Bell Tower, 1999.

Beston, Henry. *The Outermost House: A Year of Life on the Great Beach of Cape Cod*. New York: Doubleday, 1928.

Brooks, Paul. *The House of Life: Rachel Carson at Work*. Boston: Houghton Mifflin Harcourt, 1989.

Buell, Lawrence. *The Environmental Imagination: Thoreau, Nature Writing, and the Formation of American Culture*. Cambridge, MA: The Belknap Press of Harvard University Press, 1995.

Burroughs, John. *Birds and Bees, Sharp Eyes and Other Papers*. Boston: Houghton Mifflin, 1887.

———. *Journal, 1884–1885*, and *1876–1880*. http://specialcollections.vassar.edu/findingaids/burroughs_john.html.

———. *Time and Change*. Boston: Houghton Mifflin, 1912.

———. *Ways of Nature*. Boston: Houghton Mifflin, 1905.

Carson, Rachel. *The Edge of the Sea*. Boston: Houghton Mifflin, 1955.

———. *Lost Woods: The Discovered Writing of Rachel Carson*. Edited by Linda Lear. Boston: Beacon Press, 1998.

———. *The Sea Around Us*. New York: Oxford University Press, 1951.

———. *Silent Spring*. Boston: Houghton Mifflin, 1962.

Dillard, Annie. *Pilgrim at Tinker Creek*. New York: Harper and Row, 1974.

———. *Teaching a Stone to Talk: Expeditions and Encounters*. New York: Harper and Row, 1982.

———. *Tickets to a Prayer Wheel*. Columbia: University of Missouri Press, 1974.

———[Annie Doak]. "Walden Pond and Thoreau." Master's thesis, Hollins College, 1968. Wyndham Robertson Library: Special Collections Archives.

———. *The Writing Life*. New York: Harper Perennial, 2013.

Ehrlich, Gretel. *The Solace of Open Spaces*. New York: Viking, 1985.

Eisley, Loren. *The Immense Journey: An Imaginative Naturalist Explores the Mysteries of Man and Nature*. New York: Vantage Books, 1946.

Farnsworth, John. "What Does the Desert Say?: A Rhetorical Analysis of Desert Solitaire." *Interdisciplinary Literary Studies* 12, no. 1 (2010).

Fink, Augusta. *I—Mary: A Biography of Mary Austin*. Tucson: University of Arizona Press, 1983.

Fleischner, Thomas. "Natural History and the Deep Roots of Resource Management." *Natural Resources Journal* 45 (2005): 1–13.

Fritzell, Peter A. *Nature Writing and America: Essays upon a Cultural Type*. Ames: Iowa State University Press, 1990.

Goldfarb, Ben. *Eager: The Surprising, Secret Life of Beavers and Why They Matter*. White River Junction, VT: Chelsea Green, 2018.

Harwell, Albert Brantley, Jr. "Writing the Wilderness: A Study of Henry Thoreau, John Muir, and Mary Austin." PhD diss., University of Tennessee, 1992. ProQuest.

Haupt, Lyanda Lynn. *Mozart's Starling*. New York: Little, Brown Spark, 2017.

Herndon, Jerry. "Moderate Extremism: Edward Abbey and 'The Moon-Eyed Horse.'" *Western American Literature* 16, no. 2. Lincoln: Nebraska University Press, 1981.

Jeffers, Robinson. "Hurt Hawks." *The Collected Poetry of Robinson Jeffers*. New York: Random House, 1932.

Krutch, Joseph Wood. *The Desert Year*. New York: William Sloane, 1952.

———. *Henry David Thoreau*. New York: Delta, 1965.

Lanham, J. Drew. "About" [personal website]. https://jdlanham.wixsite.com/blackbirder/about.

———. *The Home Place: Memoirs of a Colored Man's Love Affair with Nature*. Minneapolis: Milkweed, 2016.

———. *Sparrow Envy: A Field Guide to Birds and Lesser Beasts*. Spartanburg, SC: Hub City Press, 2021.

Lear, Linda. *Rachel Carson: Witness for Nature*. New York: Henry Holt and Company, 1997.

Leopold, Aldo. *Game and Fish Handbook*. Albuquerque: United States Forest Service, 1915.

———. *Game Management*. New York: Charles Scribner's Sons, 1933.

———. *A Sand County Almanac: And Sketches Here and There*. New York: Oxford University Press, 1949.

Lemire, Elise. *Black Walden: Slavery and Its Aftermath in Concord, Massachusetts*. Philadelphia: University of Pennsylvania Press, 2009.

Long, William J. *School of the Woods: Some Life Studies of Animal Instincts and Animal Training*. Boston: Ginn and Company, 1902.

Lopez, Barry Holstun. *Arctic Dreams: Imagination and Desire in a Northern Landscape*. New York: Scribner, 1986.

Lutts, Ralph H. *Nature Fakers: Wildlife, Science and Sentiment*. Charlottesville: University of Virginia Press, 2001.

Mayr, Ernst. *The Growth of Biological Thought: Diversity, Evolution, and Inheritance*. Cambridge, MA: Harvard University Press, 1982.

Meloy, Ellen. *Eating Stone: Imagination and Loss in the Wild*. New York: Vantage, 2005.

Moore, Kathleen Dean. *The Pine Island Paradox: Making Connections in a Disconnected World*. Minneapolis: Milkweed, 2011.

Oliver, Mary. *Upstream: Selected Essays*. New York: Penguin, 2016.

Plass, Gilbert. "The Carbon Dioxide Theory of Climate Change." *Tellus* 8, no. 2 (May 1956).

Prather, J., and J. Briggler. "Use of Small Caves by Anurans during a Drought Period in the Arkansas Ozarks." *Journal of Herpetology* 35, no. 4 (2001): 675–78.

Quigley, Peter, ed. *Coyote in the Maze: Tracking Edward Abbey in a World of Words.* Salt Lake City: University of Utah Press, 1988.

Ribberns, Dennis. "The Making of the *Sand County Almanac.*" In *Companion to A Sand County Almanac,* edited by J. Baird Callicott. Madison: University of Wisconsin Press, 1987.

Richardson, Bob. "Biography of Annie Dillard," http://www.anniedillard.com/biography-by-bob-richardson.html.

Russel, Sharman Apt. *Diary of a Citizen Scientist: Chasing Tiger Beetles and Other New Ways of Engaging the World.* Corvallis: Oregon State University Press, 2014.

Saverin, Diana. "The Thoreau of the Suburbs." *The Atlantic,* February 5, 2015.

Souder, William. *On a Farther Shore: The Life and Legacy of Rachel Carson.* New York: Crown, 2012.

Thoreau, Henry David. *Journal, Volume XII: 1859.* https://www.walden.org/work/journal-xii-march-2-1859-november-30-1859/.

———. *Walden; or, Life in the Woods.* Boston, 1854.

———. *A Week on the Concord and Merrimack Rivers.* Boston, 1849.

Toohey, Michelle Campbell. "Remembering the Coyote." In *Exploring Lost Borders: Critical Essays on Mary Austin,* edited by Melody Graulich and Elizabeth Klimasmith. Reno: University of Nevada Press, 1999.

Walker, Brett L. *The Lost Wolves of Japan.* Seattle: University of Washington Press, 2005.

White, Gilbert. *The Natural History and Antiquities of Selborne.* London, 1789.

Williams, Terry Tempest. *Red: Passion and Patience in the Desert.* New York: Vintage, 2002.

———. *Refuge: An Unnatural History of Family and Place.* New York: Vintage, 1991.

———. *When Women Were Birds: Fifty-Four Variations on Voice.* New York: Farrar, Straus and Giroux, 2012.

———. "Writer and Naturalist-in Residence at the Utah Museum of Natural History Terry Tempest Williams." By Terry Gross. *Fresh Air from WHYY,* NPR (October 1, 1992): https://www.npr.org/1994/12/28/1108148/writer-and-naturalist-in-residence-at-the-utah-museum-of-natural-history-terry-t.

Zwinger, Ann. *Run, River, Run: A Naturalists Journey Down One of the Great Rivers of the West.* New York: HarperCollins, 1975.

Readings for Further Study, by Chapter

Walden; or, Life in the Woods by Henry David Thoreau (1854)

Balthrop-Lewis, Alda. *Thoreau's Religion: Walden Woods, Social Justice, and the Politics of Asceticism*. Cambridge, UK: Cambridge University Press, 2021.

Primrack, Richard. *Walden Warming: Climate Change Comes to Thoreau's Woods*. Chicago: University of Chicago Press, 2014.

Robinson, David M. *Natural Life: Thoreau's Worldly Transcendentalism*. Ithaca, NY: Cornell University Press, 2004

Sattelmeyer, Robert. "Walden: Climbing the Canon." *Nineteenth-Century Prose* 31, no. 2 (2004): 12–31.

Thorston, Robert M. *Walden's Shore: Henry David Thoreau and Nineteenth-Century Science*. Cambridge, MA: Harvard University Press, 2015.

Land of Little Rain by Mary Austin (1903)

Applegarth, Risa. "Genre, Location, and Mary Austin's Ethos." *Rhetoric Society Quarterly* 41 (2011): 41–63.

Bolinder, Matthew. "Appropriated Waters: Austin's Revision of Thoreau in *The Land of Little Rain*." In *Such News of the Land: U.S. Women Nature Writers*, edited by T. S. Edwards, E.A. DeWolfe, and V. Norwood, 37–46. Hanover, NH: University Press of New England, 2001.

Graulich, Melody, and Elizabeth Klimasmith, eds. *Exploring Lost Borders: Critical Essays on Mary Austin*. Reno, NV: University of Nevada Press, 1999.

Hume, Beverly A. "Austin's Consuming 'Desertness' in *The Land of Little Rain*." *Arizona Quarterly* 68, no. 4 (2012): 61–77.

Schaefer, Heike. *Mary Austin's Regionalism: Reflections on Gender, Genre, and Geography*. Charlottesville: University of Virginia Press, 2004.

Ways of Nature by John Burroughs (1905)

Buckley, Michael. "The Footsteps of Creative Energy: John Burroughs and Nineteenth-Century Literary Natural History." *American Transcendental Quarterly* 21, no. 4 (December 2007): 261–72, 301.

Lupfer, Eric. "Becoming America's 'Prophet of Outdoordom': John Burroughs and the Profession of Nature Writing, 1856–1880." *Texas Studies in Literature and Language* 52, no. 4 (Winter 2010): 381–407.

Lutts, Ralph H. *The Nature Fakers: Wildlife, Science and Sentiment*. Charlottesville: University of Virginia Press, 2001.

Mercier, Stephen M. "John Burroughs and the Nineteenth Century." *American Transcendental Quarterly* 21, no. 3 (September 2007): 151–64.

Walker, Charlotte Z., ed. *Sharp Eyes: John Burroughs and American Nature Writing*. Syracuse, NY: Syracuse University Press, 2000.

A Sand County Almanac: And Sketches Here and There by Aldo Leopold (1949)

Flader, Susan B. *Thinking Like a Mountain: Aldo Leopold and the Evolution of an Ecological Attitude toward Deer, Wolves, and Forests*. Madison: University of Wisconsin Press, 1994.

Leopold, Aldo. *The River of the Mother of God: And other Essays by Aldo Leopold*. Edited by Susan L. Flader and J. Baird Callicott. Madison: University of Wisconsin Press, 1991.

Meine, Curt D. *Aldo Leopold: His Life and His Work*. Madison: University of Wisconsin Press, 1988.

Rogers, Tim B. "Revisioning Our Views of Nature through an Examination of Aldo Leopold's *Sand County Almanac.*" *Interdisciplinary Studies in Literature and Environment* 10, no. 2 (Summer 2003): 47–73.

Warren, Julianne Lutz. *Aldo Leopold's Odyssey: Tenth Anniversary Edition.* Washington, DC: Island Press, 2016.

The Sea Around Us by Rachel Carson (1951)

Carson, Rachel. *Lost Woods: The Discovered Writing of Rachel Carson.* Edited with an introduction by Linda Lear. Boston: Beacon, 2011.

Hecht, David K. "Constructing a Scientist: Expert Authority and Public Images of Rachel Carson." *Historical Studies in the Natural Sciences* 41, no. 3 (Summer 2011): 277–302.

Kroll, Gary. "Rachel Carson's *The Sea Around Us*: The Construction of Ocean Centrism." In *America's Ocean Wilderness: A Cultural History of Twentieth-Century Exploration.* Lawrence: University Press of Kansas, 2008.

Lear, Linda. *Rachel Carson: Witness for Nature.* Boston: Mariner, 2009.

Souder, William. *On a Farther Shore: The Life and Legacy of Rachel Carson.* New York: Broadway, 2012.

Desert Solitaire: A Season in the Wilderness by Edward Abbey (1968)

Bryant, Paul T. "The Structure and Unity of *Desert Solitaire.*" *Western American Literature* 28, no. 1 (Spring 1993): 3–19.

Farnsworth, J. S. "What Does the Desert Say?: A Rhetorical Analysis of *Desert Solitaire.*" *Interdisciplinary Literary Studies: A Journal of Criticism and Theory* 12, no. 1 (Fall 2010): 105–21.

Farmer, Jared. "*Desert Solitaire* and the Literary Memory of an Imagined Place." *Western American Literature* 38, no. 2 (Summer 2003): 155–70.

Morris, David C. "Celebration and Irony: The Polyphonic Voice of Edward Abbey's *Desert Solitaire.*" *Western American Literature* 28, no. 1 (Spring 1993): 221–32.

Quigley, Peter, ed. *Coyote in the Maze: Tracking Edward Abbey in a World of Words.* Salt Lake City: University of Utah Press, 1998.

Pilgrim at Tinker Creek by Annie Dillard (1974)

Cardone, Anastasia. "Where the Twin Oceans of Beauty and Horror Meet: An Aesthetic Analysis of Annie Dillard's *Pilgrim at Tinker Creek*." *Ecozon@* 7, no. 1 (2016): 85–97.

Cheney, Jim. "The Waters of Separation: Myth and Ritual in Annie Dillard's *Pilgrim at Tinker Creek*." *Journal of Feminist Studies in Religion* 6, no. 1 (Spring 1990): 41–63.

Cochoy, Nathalie. "The Imprint of the 'Now' on the Skin of Discourse: Annie Dillard's *Pilgrim at Tinker Creek*." *Revue française d'études américaines*, no. 106, Écrire la nature (December 2005), 33–49.

McIlroy, Gary. "Pilgrim at Tinker Creek and the Burden of Science." *American Literature* 59, no. 1 (March 1987): 71–84

Slovic, Scott. *Seeking Awareness in American Nature Writing: Henry Thoreau, Annie Dillard, Edward Abbey, Wendell Berry, Barry Lopez.* Salt Lake City: University of Utah Press, 1992.

Refuge: An Unnatural History of Family and Place by Terry Tempest Williams (1991)

Austin, Michael, ed. *A Voice in the Wilderness: Conversations with Terry Tempest Williams.* Logan: Utah State University Press, 2006.

Chandler, Katherine R. "Whale Song from the Desert: Refuge without Resolution and Community without Homogeneity in Terry Tempest Williams's *Refuge*." *Women's Studies* 34, no. 8 (October 2005): 655–70.

Chandler, K. R. and M. A. Goldthwaite, eds. *Surveying the Literary Landscapes of Terry Tempest Williams.* Salt Lake City: University of Utah Press, 2003.

Kircher, Cassandra. "Rethinking Dichotomies in Terry Tempest Williams's *Refuge*." *ISLE* 3, no 1 (1996): 97–113.

Williams, Terry Tempest. *When Women Were Birds: Fifty Four Variations on Voice.* New York: Sarah Crichton, 2012.

Braiding Sweetgrass: Indigenous Wisdom, Scientific Knowledge, and the Teachings of Plants by Robin Wall Kimmerer (2013)

Greenwood, David A. "Mushrooms and Sweetgrass: A Biotic Harvest of Culture and Place-Based Learning." *Journal of Environmental Education* 48, no. 3 (2017): 205–12.

Kimmerer, Robin Wall. "Learning the Grammar of Intimacy." *Anthropology of Consciousness* (2017). https://doi.org/10.1111/anoc.12081.

———. "Restoration and Reciprocity: The Contributions of Traditional Ecological Knowledge." In *Human Dimensions of Ecological Restoration*, edited by Dave Egan, Evan E. Hjerpe, and Jesse Abrams. Washington, DC: Island Press, 2011.

Tippett, Krista. "Robin Wall Kimmerer: The Intelligence of Plants." *On Being* (podcast transcription). https://onbeing.org/programs/robin-wall-kimmerer-the-intelligence-of-plants-2022/.

Webber, Elizabeth. "Everything is Breath: Critical Plant Studies' Metaphysics of Mixture." *SubStance* 52, no. 1 (2023): 117–24.

The Home Place: Memoirs of a Colored Man's Love Affair with Nature by J. Drew Lanham (2016)

Case, Jennifer. "Place Studies: Theory and Practice in Environmental Nonfiction." *Assay* 4, no. 1 (2017).

Heitman, Danny. "Soaring High: As an Ornithologist and Writer, Drew Lanham Bridges Science and the Sensual." *Phi Kappa Phi Forum* 103, no. 2 (Summer 2023): 8–10.

Lanham, J. Drew. "Elegy in Three Plagues." *Places*, December 2020. https://placesjournal.org/article/elegy-in-three-plagues-birding-while-black/?cn-reloaded=1.

Pharr, L. D., and J. D. Lanham. "The Hopeful 'Black Birder': Living Vicariously through Birds." *Bulletin of the Ecological Society of America* 104, no. 2 (April 2023): 1–7.

Wright, Amy. "A Review of J. Drew Lanham's *The Home Place: Memoirs of a Colored Man's Love Affair with Nature*." *Brevity* (January 2017). https://brevitymag.com/book-reviews/lanham/.